Schaumburg Township District Library

130 South Roselle Road

Schaumburg, Illinois 60193

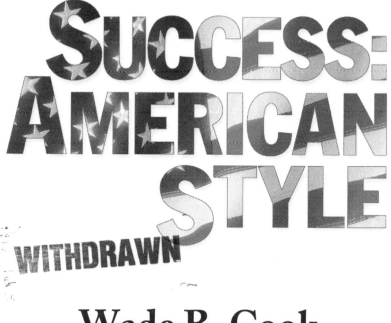

SUCCESS: AMERICAN STYLE

WITHDRAWN

Wade B. Cook

Lighthouse Publishing Group, Inc.
Seattle, Washington

Printed in the United States of America

Distributed to the trade by Origin Book Sales, Inc.
1-888-467-4446

Copyright © 2000 N.E.W., Limited Partnership

Printed in the United States of America.

ISBN 1-892008-63-7 (pbk.)

"This publication is designed to provide accurate and authoritative information in regard to the subject matter covered. It is sold with the understanding that the publisher is not engaged in rendering legal, accounting, or other professional service, and is not intended to take the place of such services or advice. If legal advice or other expert assistance is required, the services of a competent professional person should be sought."

— From a declaration of principles jointly adopted by a committee of the American Bar Association and the committee of the Publisher's Association.

Cover Design by Mark Engelbrecht
Book Design and Layout by Brent Magarrell

Published by
Lighthouse Publishing Group, Inc.
14675 Interurban Avenue South
Seattle, Washington 98168-4664
(206) 901-3000
(206) 901-3170, fax
1-800-872-7411
www.wadecook.com
www.lighthousebooks.com

Source Code: SAS00
10 9 8 7 6 5 4 3 2

Acknowledgments

I love this country and am fortunate to have friends and family who feel likewise. Thanks go to Angela Johnson, Cindy Little, Mark Engelbrecht, Bethany McVannel, Matt Krein, Tera Leonard, Larry Keim, and Brent Magarrell for helping with this book.

Patsy and Carl Sanders, Cindy Britten, Carla Norris, Debbie Losse, and Robin Anderson do so much that special grateful thanks go to them.

To my Mom and Dad, Carl and Helen Cook, and to Laura's parents Charles and Sue, I thank you for your years of dedicated service and unfeigned love.

I also thank my seminar students and teachers who give suggestions and encouragement.

Many have supplied these quotes and stories. Thanks to Stephen Bird, Senator Orrin Hatch, and Paul H. Dunn (in memorim) for their timely and well-thought-out contributions.

There are so many wonderful employees at our company, Stock Market Institute of Learning, who love this country and are passionate and patriotic.

Words cannot express the appreciation for my lovely wife, Laura. I do thank her and all of my family.

Dedication

To Laura:

One fine spring day in 1998 I found myself with Orrin Hatch, U.S. Senator from Utah. We had become fast friends, much because of our mutual love for music. He asked if he could write a song for my sweetheart. I was excited. He asked that I send him my endearing thoughts of Laura—what she means to me and why we are so close. I sent a page full of notes and he wrote the wonderful words on the following page.

Laura, you mean the world to me and I thank you for all you do. You are very special and I know you are a chosen daughter of our Heavenly Father. I am proud and honored to be your husband.

You Walk Beside Me

(For Laura Cook)
Words by Orrin G. Hatch, ASCAP
Music by Madeline Stone
Song by Natalie Grant

You're here in my heart
You're the light that guides me through the dark
You walk beside me
The night seems cold
Each time I fall, your arms are there to hold

You walk beside me
Giving strength I've never known
I am not alone,
You walk beside me

You're here in my mind,
I talk to you and all my fears unwind
I know I'm loved for who I am
You make me want to be the best I can

I must have tried your patience,
Because I know I've crossed that line
But because of you, I am…
I am not alone

In the sun, in the rain
Through the good times, and in the pain,
You're always beside me
I know that you understand
You walk beside me

Other books by Wade B. Cook:

101 Ways To Buy Real Estate Without Cash
Cook's Book On Creative Real Estate
How To Pick Up Foreclosures
Owner Financing
Real Estate For Real People
Real Estate Money Machine

Wall Street Money Machine, Volume 1
Stock Market Miracles
Safety 1st Investing

Brilliant Deductions
Wealth 101

A+
Business Buy The Bible
Don't Set Goals (The Old Way)
Wade Cook's Power Quotes, Volume 1

Y2K Gold Rush

Contents

Preface

Dallas is not usually very cold in December. The wind blowing up from the Texas plains made it seem colder than it really was. I went for a ride to check out the city and see all the new construction. Dallas was free enterprise at work in spite of the wind and cold.

This morning, on the anniversary of Pearl Harbor, the "day of infamy," the day America was drug into the Pacific Theatre of the Second World War. The tribute to our fighting forces, our involvement and the ravages of war were present throughout the day, albeit not that extensive. I was moved.

I was there to keynote the Semper Financial Convention. I had a chance to meet and visit with students who had attended my seminars. It was so wonderful. These people were on fire. Their stories still resonate in my ears and in my soul. They are experiencing their own American Dream.

Success American Style

A seed was planted. For years I have collected sayings—maxims, speeches, quotations, and such about America. These sayings range from success to families, from quality of life to Biblical scriptures and statements. I found myself repeatedly drawn to quotations about our country and about the Bible. This American category makes up a big part of my collection. Christmas was just around the corner and I wanted to put these statements together and share them with family, my friends, and employees, and with my students. You are holding the result of this endeavor.

In one short week we gathered, categorized, and typeset all of these varied writings. I sincerely hope you and your families enjoy them.

A few people on my staff are younger. As they read and typed for this book many of them were moved. They wouldn't go home. These words of our forefathers had an impact on them. It was exciting and gratifying to see the influences these inspired messages bring. These people are between the ages of 25 and 35, and many of these quotations and lessons were not taught or used in their schools.

Indeed, many great works and words of the people who built and shaped our country are not in wide use today. These words are meaningful. I mean truly meaningful—with deep thought, specific grammar written or said in powerful ways. They are worthy of study, of pondering, even of memorizing.

Sprinkled throughout this book will be scriptures and spiritual thoughts. I firmly believe that this country was kept for this time in God's purpose. People were led here. People with strength, with a desire for freedom and a willingness to pay any price to serve God and their fellow citizens.

These men and women with God's inspiration produced documents, laws, and finally a nation like no other. Let freedom ring.

The results of this yearning and churning tempered, like strong metal, a unique people. Yankees. Good people do good things. Great people produce and do great things. If we want great results in our life then why not begin at our roots and study, then ponder, then employ characteristics of great people. I contend it starts with God and distills down to all like the dews from the skies.

Our country was destined for greatness, but it can only remain great if we as a people do good works and do great things.

God bless us in this best of enterprises.

We have included a very special report by Wade Cook in the appendix of this book. While the general objective of this book is to underscore the greatness of America, one of the things that comes to mind is that this is indeed the land of opportunity. Yes, the American Dream is alive and well, and still has room for more participants.

The special report in the back of this book draws some powerful correlations between America's favorite pastime (baseball) and the stock market. Be sure to carefully read this report and you'll learn some how-to-invest-in-the-stock-market strategies. This is the land of opportunity and the time is now!

We Are Adequate To The Task

(Exerpted from *Business Buy the Bible*, by Wade B. Cook)

What twisted path of logic
must our mind walk down
to bring on fear of achieving?
Life has an abundance to offer,
and we are not inadequate to the task.
Innate to our souls is an endless power
to innervate all things around us,
and to possess all good things
through noble endeavor.
A kind and wise God has equipped us
with all that we need to find joy here
and in His world.
We have to think of lofty ways
to inspire our life.
We owe Him no less,
for truly, we can say He is our Father
and we, his children.

Wade B. Cook

1
A Great Country

For years I have felt a humble gratitude to God for allowing me the unspeakable blessing of being born in this country. My career, which hase been filled with opportunities of helping people, is probably singular to this country. Where else would anyone enjoy the freedom to take full advantage of the laws, free enterprise and the history of achievement—of people living and striving to achieve their American Dream?

I discovered a deep and abiding vein of truth running through virtually every American—a knowledge, if you will, that anyone can achieve greatness. A sort of "anyone can grow up and become president" mentality. It's wonderful. I often ponder this aspect of our shared lives. We find it everywhere.

So, I question, where does this idea come from? From our parents? From good teachers? From great leaders? Maybe it comes from the wisdom and thoughts of our Founding Fathers. Oh, I thought I was getting close, but my research led me along and I found the quotations in this chapter. You will find here the true source of all good.

Then it was said among the nations, "The Lord has done great things for them." The Lord has done great things for us, and we are filled with joy.

~Psalms 126:2-3

O Lord, Almighty and everlasting God, by Thy Word Thou hast created the heaven, and the earth, and the sea; blessed and glorified be Thy Name, and praised be Thy Majesty, which hath deigned to use us, Thy humble servants, that Thy holy Name may be proclaimed in this second part of the earth.

~Christopher Columbus

No one should fear to undertake any task in the name of our Saviour, if it is just and if the intentions are purely for His holy service. The working out of all things has been assigned to each person by our Lord, but it all happens according to His sovereign will even though He gives advice.

~Christopher Columbus

It must be felt that there is no national security but in the nation's humble acknowledged dependence upon God and His overruling providence.

~President John Adams

I shall look for whatever success may attend my public service; and knowing that "except the Lord keep the city the watchman waketh but in vain," with fervent supplications for His favor, to His overruling providence I commit with humble but fearless confidence my own fate and the future destinies of my country.

~John Quincy Adams

I assume the arduous and responsible duties of President of the United States, relying upon the support of my countrymen and invoking the guidance of Almighty God.

~William McKinley

A Great Country

In the beginning of the contest with Great Britain, when we were sensible of danger, we had daily prayers in this room for divine protection. Our prayers were heard, and they were graciously answered...Have we now forgotten this powerful friend? Or do we no longer need his assistance?

I have lived a long time, and the longer I live, the more convincing the proofs I see of this truth: "that God governs the affairs of man." And if a sparrow cannot fall to the ground without his notice, is it probable that an empire can rise without his aid?

~Ben Franklin to the Constitutional Congress 1787

I appear, my fellow-citizens, in your presence and in that of Heaven to bind myself by the solemnities of religious obligation to the faithful performance of the duties alotted to me in the station to which I have been called.

~John Quincy Adams

While this duty rests upon me I shall do my utmost to speak their purpose and to do their will, seeking Divine guidance to help us each and every one to give light to them that sit in darkness and to guide our feet into the way of peace.

~Franklin D. Roosevelt

We are faced with the responsibility of either choosing God or denying him, but God wants America to repent and return to Him, to love Him with all our hearts, and to love one another.

~James Kennedy

With a firm reliance on the protection of the Almighty God, I shall forthwith commence the duties of the high trust to which you have called me.

~James Monroe

Success American Style

America seeks no earthly empire built on blood and force. No ambition, no temptation, lures her to thought of foreign dominions. The legions which she sends forth are armed, not with the sword, but with the cross. The higher state to which she seeks the allegiance of all mankind is not of human, but of divine origin. She cherishes no purpose save to merit the favor of Almighty God.

~Calvin Coolidge

Before all else, we seek, upon our common labor as a nation, the blessings of Almighty God.

~Dwight D. Eisenhower

Above all, I know there is a Supreme Being who rules the affairs of men and whose goodness and mercy have always followed the American people and I know He will not turn from us now if we humbly and reverently seek His powerful aid.

~Grover Cleveland

In the presence of my countrymen, mindful of the solemnity of this occasion, knowing what the task means and the responsibility which it involves, I beg your tolerance, your aid, and your cooperation. I ask the help of Almighty God in this service to my country to which you have called me.

~Herbert Hoover

We ought to cultivate peace, commerce, and friendship with all nations, and this is not merely the best means of promoting our own material interests, but in a spirit of Christian benevolence toward our fellow-men, wherever their lot may be cast.

~James Buchanan

I only look to the gracious protection of the Divine Being whose strengthening support I humbly solicit, and whom I fervently pray to look down upon us all.

~Martin Van Buren

A Great Country

The unselfishness of these United States is a thing proven; our devotion to peace for ourselves and for the world is well established; our concern for preserved civilization has had its impassioned and heroic expression.

~Warren G. Harding

The church was and is the foundation of our community. It became our strength, our refuge, and our haven.

~Rosa Parks

The great essential to our happiness and prosperity is that we adhere to the principles upon which the Government was established and insist upon their faithful observance.

~William McKinley

God loves America. When you consider what He went through to bring our forebearers to this magnificent land, and when you realize what He accomplished in bringing forth a new nation on this continent - a government founded on Christian principles and dedicated to life, liberty, and the pursuit of happiness - you have to realize that He had a dramatic vision and purpose for this nation.

~James Kennedy

And by the blessing of God may that country itself become a vast and splendid monument, not of oppression and terror, but of wisdom, of peace, and of liberty, upon which the world may gaze with admiration, forever.

~Daniel Webster

God reigns over the nations; God sits upon the throne of his holiness.

~Psalms 47:8

Success American Style

It is the duty of nations, as well as of men, to own their dependence upon the overruling power of God and to recognize the sublime truth announced in the Holy Scriptures and proven by all history, that those nations only are blessed whose God is the Lord.

~Abraham Lincoln

I do, therefore, invite my fellow citizens in every part of the United States...to set apart and observe the last Thursday of November next as a day of Thanksgiving and Praise to our beneficent Father who dwelleth in the heavens...[it is] announced in the Holy Scriptures and proven by all history, that those nations are blessed whose God is the Lord...It has seemed to me fit and proper that God should be solemnly, reverently and gratefully acknowledged, as with one heart and one voice, by the whole American people.

~Abraham Lincoln

My fellow-citizens, no people on earth have more cause to be thankful than ours, and this is said reverently, in no spirit of boastfulness in our own strength, but with gratitude to the Giver of Good who has blessed us with the conditions which have enabled us to achieve so large a measure of well-being and of happiness.

~Theodore Roosevelt

To the influence of this Book we are indebted for all the progress made in true civilization.

~Ulysses S. Grant

America's record in this century has been unparalleled in the world's history for its responsibility, for its generosity, for its creativity, and for its progress.

~Richard Nixon

The Lord brings the counsel of the nations to nothing; he frustrates the plans of the peoples. The counsel of the Lord stands forever, the thoughts of his heart to all generations. Blessed is the nation whose God is the Lord, and the people he has chosen for his inheritance, The Lord looks from heaven; he beholds all the sons of men. From the place of his habitation he looks upon al the inhabitants of the earth. He fashions their hearts alike; he observes all their deeds. There is no king saved by the multitude of an army; a mighty man is not delivered by great strength.

~Psalms 33:10-16

The God who gave us life gave us liberty at the same time.

~Thomas Jefferson

In the swift rush of great events, we find ourselves groping to know the full sense and meaning of these times in which we live. In our quest of understanding, we beseech God's guidance.

~Dwight D. Eisenhower

With a firm reliance on the protection of Almighty God, I shall forthwith commence the duties of the high trust to which you have called me.

~James Monroe

I deem the present occasion sufficiently important and solemn to justify me in expressing to my fellow-citizens a profound reverence for the Christian religion and a thorough conviction that sound morals, religious liberty, and a just sense of religious responsibility are essentially connected with all true and lasting happiness.

~William Henry Harrison

No country is more loved by its people. I have an abiding faith in their capacity, integrity, and high purpose.

~Herbert Hoover

7

Success American Style

Let us go forth to lead the land we love, asking His blessing and His help, but knowing that here on earth God's work must truly be our own.

~John F. Kennedy

I accept my part with single-mindedness of purpose and humility of spirit, and implore the favor and guidance of God in His Heaven.

~Warren G. Harding

We Americans of today, together with our allies, are passing through a period of supreme test. It is a test of our courage - of our resolve - of our wisdom - our essential democracy.

~Franklin D. Roosevelt

I have been driven many times upon my knees by the overwhelming conviction that I had nowhere else to go. My own wisdom, and that of all about me, seemed insufficient for that day.

~Abraham Lincoln

It is the duty of nations, as well as of men, to owe their dependence upon the overruling power of God and to recognize the sublime truth announced in the holy scriptures and proven by all history, that those nations only are blessed whose God is the Lord.

~Abraham Lincoln

America, the Beautiful

O beautiful for spacious skies,
For amber waves of grain,
For purple mountain majesties
Above the fruited plain!
America! America! God shed His grace on thee,
And crown they good with brotherhood
From sea to shining sea.

O beautiful for heroes proved
In liberating strife,
Who more than self their country loved
And mercy more than life!
America! America! May God thy gold refine,
Till all success be nobleness,
And ev'ry gain divine.

O beautiful for patriot dream
That sees, beyond the years,
Thine alabaster cities gleam -
Undimmed by human tears!
America! America! God shed His grace on thee,
And crown thy good with brotherhood
From sea to shining sea.

~Katherine Lee Bates

2
Heal Our Land

Throughout our nation's history, prayers have risen to God to bless our land, our families and our endeavors. I find it amazing that words spoken to God are often blessed by God himself—they are more eloquent, more thoughtful, indeed even more sublime.

I hope in presenting the following quotations that there develops within you a stronger desire to return to God's words and to his ways. I hope we share his words with our children and instill these great scriptures, maxims and citations with them.

Read the Jewish Shema - Hear, O Israel:

Hear, O Israel: The Lord our God is one Lord: And thou shalt love the Lord thy God with all thine heart, and with all thy soul, and with all thy might.

Deuteronomy 6:4-5

And this continues on:

And these words, which I command thee this day, shall be in thine heart: And thou shalt teach them diligently unto thy children, and shalt talk to them when thou sittest in thine house, and when thou walkest by the way, and when thou liest down, and when thou risest up.

~Deuteronomy 6:6-7

In addition, we are commanded to love one another:

Thou shalt not avenge, nor bear any grudge against the children of thy people, but thou shalt love thy neighbour as thyself: I am the Lord.

~Leviticus 19:18

These are two great commandments.

Remember when Jesus was questioned by the lawyer, and then at another time by the scribe? What wonderful responses! I'll list the first account:

...Thou shalt love the Lord thy God with all thy heart, and with all thy soul, and with all thy mind. This is the first and great commandment. And the second is like unto it, Thou shalt love thy neighbor as thyself. On these two commandments hang all the law and the prophets.

~Matthew 22:37-40

Do nothing out of selfish ambition or vain conceit, but in humility consider others better than yourselves. Each of you should look not only to your own interests, but also to the interests of others.

~Philippians 2:3-4 (NIV)

To these scriptures add the following inspirational thoughts about our country—the Bible, God's ways, and we have a course for living.

May I add to these thoughts a simple adjunct: We too need healing. In Hebrew the same root word exists for heal, whole and holy. (See *A+* by Wade Cook for more on this). The concept is simple. God is whole, He is undivided. He is One. For us to be healed, individually and as a country, we must seek to be Holy, as He is.

I hope these thoughtful quotations help in your endeavors.

Our deepest fear is not that we are inadequate. Our deepest fear is that we are powerful beyond measure. It is our light, not our darkness, that most frightens us. We ask ourselves, who am I to be brilliant, gorgeous, talented, and fabulous? Actually, who are you not to be? You are a child of God. Your playing small doesn't serve the world. There is nothing enlightened about shirnking so that other people won't feel insecure around you. We are born to make manifest the Glory of God that is within us. It's not just in some of us, it's in everyone, and as we let our own light shine, we consciously give other people permission to do the same. As we are liberated from our own fear, our presence automatically liberates others.

~Nelson Mandela, President of South Africa

Heal Our Land

Heal our land.
Please grant us peace today,
and strengthen all who lack the faith
to call on thee each day.
Heal our land,
and keep us safe and free.
Watch over all who understand
the need for liberty.

Heal our land and guide us with Thy hand.
Heal our land and help us understand
that we must put our trust in Thee
if we would be free.

Heal our land.
Please help us find our way,
for in Thy word we find our strength
if we look up each day.
Heal our land,
and fill us with Thy love.
Keep us upon the path of truth
that comes from heav'n above.

Heal our land and guide us with Thy hand.
Heal our land and help us understand
that we must put our trust in Thee
if we would be free.

Protect us by the power of Thy rod,
and keep us as one nation under God.
Heal our land, heal our land,
and guide us with Thy hand

~Senator Orrin Hatch

Our Father, bring to the remembrance of Thy people Thine ancient and time-honored promise: "If my people, which are called by my name, shall humble themselves, and pray, and seek my face, and turn from their wicked ways; then will I hear from Heaven, and will forgive their sin, and will heal their land."

We - This company of Thy people assembled - would begin now to meet the conditions that will enable Thee to fulfill Thy promise.

May all of America come to understand that right-living alone exalteth a nation, that only in Thy will can peace and joy be found. But, Lord, this land cannot be righteous unless her people are righteous, and we, here gathered, are part of America. We know that the world cannot be changed until the hearts of men are changed. Our hearts need to be changed.

We therefore confess to Thee that:

Wrong ideas and sinful living have cut us off from Thee.

We have been greedy.

We have sought to hide behind barricades of selfishness; shackles have imprisoned the great heart of America.

We have tried to isolate ourselves from the bleeding wounds of a blundering world.

In our self-sufficiency we have sought not thy help.

We have held conferences and ignored Thee completely.

~Peter Marshall

And may that Infinite Power which rules the destinies of the universe lead our councils to what is best, and give them a favorable issue for your peace and prosperity.

~Thomas Jefferson

Success American Style

I urge each man and woman...to declare before God that you will do your part – to swear by the power of God's indwelling presence that, from this day forward, you will do more to get the Gospel to other people – that you will do more than you've ever done before to speak up for the values and beliefs upon which our nation was founded.

~James Kennedy

America is ready to encourage, eager to initiate, and promote that brotherhood of mankind which must be God's highest conception of human relationship.

~Warren G. Harding

There is no solid basis for civilization but in the Word of God. If we abide by the principles taught in the Bible, our country will go on prospering...I make it a practice to read the Bible through once every year.

~Daniel Webster

There is nothing wrong with America that the faith, love of freedom, intelligence and energy of her citizens cannot cure.

~Dwight D. Eisenhower

My eyes will be on the faithful in the land, that they may dwell with me; he whose walk is blameless will minister to me.

~Psalms 101:6

I think patriotism is like charity – it begins at home.

~Henry James

God has given you your country as cradle, and humanity as mother; you cannot rightly love your brethren of the cradle if you love not the common mother.

~Giuseppe Mazzini

Our ancestors established their system of government on morality and religious sentiment. Moral habits, they believed, cannot safely be trusted on any other foundation than religious principle, nor any government be secure which is not supported by moral habits...Whatever makes men good Christians, makes them good citizens.

~Daniel Webster, at the bicentennial celebration of the landing of the Pilgrims at Plymouth Rock. December 22, 1820

If we remember that God loves us and that we can love others as he loves us, then America can become the sign of peace for the whole world, the sign of joy from where a sign of care for the weakest and the weak, the unborn child, must go out to the world. If you become a burning light of justice and peace in the world, then really you will be true to what the founders of this country stood for. This is to love one another as God loves each one of us. And where does this love begin? In our own home. How does it begin? By praying together.

~Mother Teresa

My great passion for America is twofold: first, that every believer would be absolutely faithful to the Great Commission; and then, that every believer would take seriously the challenge to reclaim this nation for Christ. If we become engaged and if we carry out the "cultural mandate" of the church, then there is no reason that we cannot reclaim our heritage of faith and freedom and see this nation renewed.

~James Kennedy

Entering thus solemnly into covenant with each other, we may reverently invoke and confidently expect the favor and help of Almighty God - that He will give to me wisdom, strength, and fidelity, and to our people a spirit of fraternity and a love of righteousness and peace.

~Benjamin Harrison

17

This occasion is not alone in the administration of the most sacred oath which can be assumed by an American citizen. It is a dedication and consecration under God to the highest office in service of our people. I assume this trust in the humility of knowledge that only through the guidance of Almighty Providence can I hope to discharge its ever-increasing burdens.

~Herbert Hoover

We know, our Father, that at this desperate hour in world affairs, we need thee. We need thy strength, thy guidance, thy wisdom. There are problems far greater than any wisdom of man can solve. What shall our leaders do in such an hour?

May thy wisdom and thy power come upon those whom have been entrusted leadership. May the responsibility lie heavily on their hearts, until they are ready to acknowledge their helplessness and turn to thee. Give to them the honesty, the courage, and the moral integrity to confess that they don't know what they do. Only then can they lead us as a nation beyond human wisdom to thee, who alone hast the answer.

Lead us to this high adventure. Remind us that a "mighty fortress is our God" - not a hiding place where we can escape for an easy life, but rather an arsenal of courage and strength the mightiest of all, who will march beside us into the battle for righteousness and world brotherhood.

~Peter Marshall

If my people, which are called by my name, shall humble themselves and pray and seek my face and turn from their wicked ways, then will I hear from heaven, and will forgive their sin, and will heal their land.

~2 Chronicles 7:14

Righteousness exalts a nation, but sin is a reproach to any people.

~Proverbs 14:34

Where there is no vision, the people perish.

~Proverbs 29:18

I always say that the studious perusal of the Sacred Volume will make better citizens, better fathers, and better husbands.

~Thomas Jefferson

Rob not the poor, because he is poor: neither oppress the afflicted in the gate: For the Lord will plead their cause, and spoil the soul of those that spoiled them.

~Proverbs 22:22-23

To pray effectively we must want what God wants - that and only that is to pray in the will of God. And no petition made in the will of God was ever refused.

~A. W. Tozer

We must wait on Him moment by moment for the fulfillment of His promised blessings and must trust Him to obtain them for us. So that in a fuller sense than ever before we are nothing and Christ is all. The only prayer that accomplishes anything is that which was offered in "the power and reality of the life of Christ in the soul." The Spirit must make intercession in us, if we expect to have power with God.

~Hannah Whitall Smith

The faith we bring to prayer must include a trust that God is able to hear our prayers and that He is disposed to answer them. Yet when God says no to our requests, this faith also trusts in His wisdom.

~R. C. Sproul

Success American Style

O God, our Father, we pray that the people of America, who have made such progress in material things, may now seek to grow in spiritual understanding.

For we have improved means, but not improved ends. We have better ways of getting there, but we have no better places to go. We can save more time, but are not making any better use of the time we save.

We need Thy help to do something about the world's true problems - the problem of lying, which is called propaganda; the problem of selfishness, which is called self-interest; the problem of greed, which is often called profit; the problem of license disguising itself as liberty; the problem of lust, masquerading as love; the problem of materialism, the hook which is baited with security.

Hear our prayers, O Lord, for the spiritual understanding which is better than political wisdom, that we may see our problems for what they are. This we ask in Jesus' name, Amen.

~Peter Marshall

Give, and it shall be given to you. A good measure, pressed down, shaken together and running over, will be poured into your lap. For with the measure you use, it will be measured to you.

~Luke 6:38

When I seek to point people to Christ, it is because I am convinced that He alone is God's answer to life's deepest problems. I have seen Him bring change in the lives of countless individuals who have turned to Him in true repentance and faith. One of the New Testament's most compelling images of spiritual conversion is found in the phrase born again or new birth...We need what Jesus was teaching: a spiritual rebirth or renewal from within, by the power of God...It takes place as we turn in faith to Christ and submit ourselves to Him. God Himself takes up residence in our lives through His Holy Spirit.

~Billy Graham

3
Freedom—How Rare A Possession

From the forthcoming book *Finding Freedom*
by Stephen M. Bird
Copyright © 1999 Stephen M. Bird
Used by permission.

Two teenagers who survived the Columbine High School massacre "recounted their stories in the sanctuary of the First Baptist Church." Seth Houy reported that "Harris and Klebold moved closer and closer to him as they continued to aim and fire, all the while laughing and making fun of the students they killed. 'They told everyone they've wanted to do this all their lives,' he said."[1] Erika Dendorfer said that the two killers "just opened their hearts to evil that day. I believe it was a spiritual battle."[2]

Is Erika right? Was it a spiritual battle? Had they "just opened their hearts to evil?" Considering that the violence at Columbine High School launched a national debate on the relevance of the Second Amendment, will we lose any of our freedoms? What is the media contributing to this violence? Are there deeper causes? How is this violence connected to the discussion of religious faith in the public square? Is the war to discuss and profess our religious faith publicly-

Success American Style

America's Real War, as identified by Rabbi Daniel Lapin? And if so, what are some of the consequences if people of religious faith lose this war to persons of secular faith?

How important is religious faith, or lack of it, to our families, our communities, our nation? As a nation, could this collective rise in violence across America be occurring as we suffer from a collective decline in the public expressions of our religious faith? If so, how will that affect the peace and prosperity we have enjoyed? How will that affect our civilization? Could we lose it? After all, civilization is fragile, and rarely achieved. C. S. Lewis said

"One of the most dangerous errors instilled into us by nineteenth-century progressive optimism is the idea that civilization is automatically bound to increase and spread. The lesson of history is the opposite; civilization is a rarity, attained with difficulty and easily lost. The normal state of humanity is barbarism, just as the normal surface of our planet is salt water."[3]

Progress isn't automatic. It is attained by effort, self-discipline, and self-control. Whenever that effort is generally relaxed, societies can decline and even revert to barbarism. This has been demonstrated clearly in our modern times. Zbigniew Brzezinski, former director of the National Security Council, said that the "onset of the twentieth century was hailed in many commentaries as the real beginning of the Age of Reason." Then he chronicled the barbarism of this century, listing "two world wars and at least thirty additional major international or civil wars." After reviewing the atrocities, he noted that at least 167 million people were slaughtered through deliberate political action. "This is more than the total killed in all previous wars, civil conflicts, and religious persecutions throughout human history."[4]

Imagine the suffering of those who lived through the wars and concentration camps. Yet all this evil was done in the twentieth century, the most technologically advanced century in history, the century we like to think of as the greatest in human history; the dawning of the Age of Reason. Such is the fragility of civilized behavior. It is hard to develop and easily lost.

Freedom—How Rare A Possession

I recently spoke with friends, Dean and Ann Richards who own their own business, Richards Laboratories, and who left it for a time to provide humanitarian service in Indonesia which has a population of about 220 million people. They lived in Bogor, Java for more than two years and became well acquainted with the people. They dug wells and provided pumps for medical clinics. They obtained tons of food for starving villagers. They also described incredibly primitive practices regarding hygiene and personal cleanliness.

Dean said that "in the Irian Jaya portion of New Guinea, some of the inhabitants are only one generation away from their traditional practice of headhunting and cannibalism. Their belief is that if they eat the brain of an enemy who comes against them, if they're victorious and eat the brain of their enemy, they gain the strength and the wisdom of that individual." He said that inland on the island of Java which contains 80% of the population of Indonesia, many of the villagers are still animists. They still worship trees, rocks, and wooden carvings, etc. and believe that witch doctors have supernatural power. Many societies today are still this backward.

Our Precious Freedom

The freedom we enjoy with our republican form of government is even more rare than civilization in general. Kings, emperors, monarchs, tsars, rulers, regents, lords, suzerains, governors, and chieftains, etc. have been virtually standard governmental fare throughout all of recorded history, and they have not usually been voted into or out of office.

Historically, we have not long held the notion that liberty is an inalienable right from God, a right that "may not be taken away."[5] Our Constitution was written just a little over two hundred years ago. This represents a period of time which is less than three and one-half percent of recorded history. How far back does history go? How many thousands of years have passed? "Tip" O'Neill, former Speaker of the House has noted that: "About two-thirds of the world's governments have constitutions drafted since 1970."[6]

Success American Style

Historically, it has been far more common to believe that liberty is not an inalienable right from God. The notions of slavery are diametrically opposed to the notions of freedom, and it has been a far more common practice to enslave people, than to liberate them. David Eltis noted that "slavery until recently was universal in two senses. Most settled societies incorporated the institution into their social structures, and few peoples in the world have not constituted a major source of slaves at one time or another."[7]

Thomas Sowell further pointed out that "slavery was in fact one of the oldest and most widespread institutions on Earth. Slavery existed in the Western Hemisphere before Columbus' ships appeared on the horizon, and it existed in Europe, Asia, Africa, and the Middle East for thousands of years. Slavery was older than Islam, Buddhism, or Christianity, and both the secular and religious moralists of societies around the world accepted human bondage, not only as a fact of life but as something requiring no special moral justification."[8] He goes on to note that slavery was "'peculiar' in the United States only because human bondage was inconsistent with the principles on which this nation was founded. Historically, however, it was those principles [of freedom] which were peculiar, not slavery."[9]

Thus we can see that while civilization itself is a rare phenomenon, democratic civilizations are rarer still. Comparatively speaking, only a handful of nations have achieved it. If you look, you will find it here in the United States, in "the United Kingdom and its dominions" and on the continent of Europe. M. Stanton Evans notes that: "To these have been added in recent years some parts of Latin America and the Pacific, and a state or two in Africa . . . That is the lot."[10]

Remember too, that modern democratic governments in this century have been lost. Hitler and his Nazi cronies toppled the German Republic. He annexed Austria, captured Czechoslovakia, crushed Poland, blitzkrieged France, and eventually overran nearly all of modern Europe. Not surprisingly, he and his friends also gave us World War II, the Holocaust, slave labor camps, and murder on a massive scale.

Lenin overthrew the provisional Russian democratic republic and shut down free elections. Stalin murdered millions of his own people; by execution or by starvation. He partitioned Eastern Europe by building a wall between East and West Berlin-imprisoning West Berlin. Between Eastern and Western Europe, he built a string of chain link fences with guard towers, guards, guard dogs, mines, machine guns etc, and he continued Hitler's practice of imprisoning nations. Our Founding Fathers accomplished something extraordinary. Warren Bennis is eminently qualified to evaluate leaders. He has been Distinguished Professor of Business Administration at the University of Southern California, and has conducted impressive research on leadership. In one of his books, *On Becoming a Leader*, he described Washington, Jefferson, Madison, Adams, Franklin and Hamilton as "six world-class leaders."[11] Then he marveled that a country with a population of only three million people could produce so many men like them. Today in America, from a population of roughly 240 million people, he would not compare any recent political leaders with them.

Barbara Tuchman, winner of two Pulitzer prizes, has been called "the most successful practicing historian in the United States today, and also the best." She has been likewise impressed. She documents in her book *The March to Folly*, the tendency of governmental officials to make dumb mistakes, but she cites our Founding Fathers as an exception to that tendency, and sides with Arthur M. Schlesinger, Sr. who called them "the most remarkable generation of public men in the history of the United States or perhaps of any other nation."[12] She went on to say that "it would be invaluable if we could know what produced this burst of talent from a base of only two and a half million inhabitants."[13] Nevertheless she had to acknowledge that our Founders' "example is too rare to be a basis of normal expectations."[14]

Considering the seemingly powerful forces operating against the building of civilizations, and especially against free governments, how do democracies arise? How are they upheld and sustained? What sort of energy and effort is required to push them forward? How can that energy be accumulated or lost?

Religion and Freedom

What was different about the founders of our nation? What was different about the culture that produced them? What was different about the colonial Americans who led out in their quest for freedom? Alexis de Tocqueville wanted to know the same thing. He was a government official in France who obtained leave without pay to visit America to research its prison system. He left France on 2 April 1831, and arrived in New York on 11 May that year, roughly forty-four years after the Constitutional Convention in Philadelphia. He spent nine months in America "investigating the beliefs and institutions of the American people, and he interviewed hundreds of them, including President Andrew Jackson."[15] In his book *Democracy in America* he noted one striking feature of America.

On my arrival in the United States the religious aspect of the country was the first thing that struck my attention; and the longer I stayed there, the more I perceived the great political consequences resulting from this new state of things.[16]

Americans were religious! Because Tocqueville was an agnostic who had lost his faith, this is an "odd" sort of thing for him to notice. His surprise at the way Americans linked liberty with religion is apparent when he writes that in France he had "almost always seen the spirit of religion and the spirit of freedom marching in opposite directions. But in America ... they were intimately united."[17]

Our Founding Fathers Believed in Religious Virtue.

Warren Bennis said that the Founding Fathers "based the Constitution on the assumption that there was such a thing as public virtue."[18] Virtue is "general moral excellence; right action and thinking." It is "goodness and morality," as well as an "effective power or force ... especially the ability to heal or strengthen"[19] It was goodness, and as political science scholar, Richard Vetterli has noted: "For Americans, the Bible was the primary source of the idea of virtue."[20] Judaic virtue is presented in the Old Testament, and one acquires its power by practicing the Ten Commandments. Christian virtue is an extension of Judaic virtue and is found in both the Old and New Testaments. Likewise, one acquires its strength by practicing it.

What did our Founding Fathers think of the importance of virtue to the continuance of freedom? They were excellent students of history and deep thinkers who created a republican national government with an unparalleled emphasis on inalienable rights which they got from the Bible. Consider the thinking of our "six world-class leaders."

It is impossible to rightly govern the world without God and the Bible.[21]

~George Washington

It is in the manners and spirit of a people which preserve a republic in vigour...degeneracy in these is a canker which soon eats into the heart of its laws and constitution.[22]

~Thomas Jefferson

We have staked the whole future of American civilization, not upon the power of government, far from it. We have staked the future of all of our political institutions...upon the capacity of each and all of us to govern ourselves, to control ourselves, to sustain ourselves according to the Ten Commandments of God.[23]

~ James Madison

[This] Form of government...is productive of every Thing which is great and excellent among Men. But its principles are as easily destroyed, as human nature is corrupted...A Government is only to be supported by pure Religion or Austere Morals. Private, and public virtue is the only Foundation of Republics.[24]

~ John Adams

Success American Style

We have no government armed with power capable of contending with human passions unbridled by morality and religion. . . . Our Constitution was made only for a moral and religious people. It is wholly inadequate to the government of any other.[25]

~John Adams

[O]nly a virtuous people are capable of freedom. As nations become corrupt and vicious, they have more need of masters.[26]

~Benjamin Franklin

He who shall introduce into public affairs the principles of primitive Christianity will change the face of the world.[27]

~Benjamin Franklin

It has been frequently remarked that it seems to have been reserved to the people of this country, by their conduct and example, to decide the important question, whether societies of men are really capable or not of establishing good government from reflection and choice, or whether they are forever destined to depend for their political constitutions on accident and force.[28]

~Alexander Hamilton

How would Americans establish good government? "By their conduct and example." Is it not self-evident that a sufficient amount of virtuous "conduct and example" are critical to the maintenance of a civilization and the establishment of a real republic? How many killers like the two at Columbine High School, can a society tolerate? How large a portion of a nation's population can it put in prisons and jails and still function effectively? How often and how frequently can leaders and citizens disregard Constitutional laws before anarchy or governance by personal will arises?

In their emphasis on virtue, our Founding Fathers were dramatically different from Lenin, Stalin and Hitler. Our Founding Fathers emphasized Judeo-Christian morals and precepts, whereas modern totalitarian tyrants rejected Judeo-Christian morals and precepts. Modern totalitarian tyrants subscribe to the theory that the ends justify the means. Tyrants believe that if their goals are good, then they can do anything to achieve them. In stark contrast, our Founding Fathers all believed that only virtuous means (i.e. virtuous methods) could be used to attain virtuous goals. They believed that building virtue in our nation's leaders and citizenry was more important than building a paradise on earth for all people.

Clearly, Hitler, Marx, Lenin, Stalin, and Mao feared too much Judeo-Christian virtue among their citizens, else why would they strive so hard to control it? They had to weaken virtue in their citizens in order to obtain obedience for their evil plans. They had to intimidate the courageous. They had to deceive the noble. They had to lie. They had to control religious thought and worship and weaken it in order to get their citizens to tolerate abuses to their consciences, or even to violate their own consciences.

Samuel Adams, sometimes called the "Father of the American Revolution," elaborated on this theme by saying: "A General Dissolution of Principles and Manners will more surely overthrow the Liberties of America than the whole Force of the Common Enemy. While the people are virtuous they cannot be subdued; but when once they lose their Virtue they will be ready to surrender their Liberties to the first external or internal Invader ... If Virtue and Knowledge are diffused among the People, they will never be enslaved. This will be their great Security."[29] Is this true? Let's test the idea.

If we go back to the example of the two killers at Columbine High School, and if we assume the importance of virtue as proposed by our "six world class leaders," we can see immediately that the main problem was not so much that the killers had obtained guns, but the main problem was that they had not obtained enough virtue to restrain their bloodthirsty desires. They could not contain their murderous glee. Being without the virtue of compassion, they cared not one whit for the rights of their classmates, nor even for their own rights. Lacking virtue, the killers stole the inalienable rights of life, liberty, and the pursuit of happiness from twelve of their classmates and a teacher. Then, of their own free will and choice, the killers shot themselves, effectively surrendering their own inalienable rights to life, liberty, and the pursuit of happiness.

Let's contrast our two young killers at Columbine with the actions of another young man. I found this in Scouting magazine. As you know the Boy Scouts of America (BSA), tries to build virtue in our young men; scouting tries to build good character. At any rate, the President of the BSA and its Chief Scout Executive wrote about "Webelos Scout Daniel Simon of Pack 381, Buffalo Grove, Ill." saying:

Last year Daniel earned a $750 gift certificate.

Instead of using the certificate to buy merchandise for himself, Daniel filled seven shopping carts with toys for other children—toys that were distributed during the Wheeling, Ill., Food Basket Drive to needy families just after Thanksgiving. The store manager was so impressed by the Webelos Scout's generosity, she contributed $300 more in gift certificates. Daniel even had a few toys left over, which he donated to area hospitals.

"He never ceases to amaze us with his generosity," said Daniel's mom, Karen, proudly. The BSA is proud of Daniel, too—and gratified that he understood so clearly the value of putting others' welfare ahead of his own.[30]

Every Boy Scout is required to memorize The Scout Law, a list of twelve virtues, similar to Benjamin Franklin's thirteen virtues. Every Boy Scout is also required to memorize the Scout Oath, which is often reaffirmed by the boys at Scout meetings.

On my honor I will do my best
To do my duty to God and my country ...;
To help other people at all times;
To keep myself ... morally straight.[31]

It seems to me that Webelos Scout Daniel Simon of Pack 381 of Buffalo Grove, Illinois has a lot to give us; something from his heart; something I call—virtue, or goodness. If he stays on this track, and should we look at his life in the future, I think we would find a successful and a happy young man. The virtue/goodness in his heart will enable him to build and lift others. Is there anyone who wonders whether or not he'll be well thought of by those around him? If you had to build a society, who would you choose to lead it? Daniel? or the killers at Columbine High School?

Edmund Burke was a great English statesman and orator who abandoned his "legal studies for literary work," but entered Parliament in 1765. He "gained high position among Whigs through eloquence" in advocating generous treatment of the American colonies. He also "supported Wilberforce in advocating [the] abolition of slave trade."[32] A deep thinker on the issues of freedom and liberty, his ideas have profound implications for men and women everywhere. He said:

Men are qualified for civil liberty in exact proportion to their disposition to put moral chains on their own appetites; in proportion as their love of justice is above their rapacity; in proportion as their soundness and sobriety of understanding is above their vanity and presumption; in proportion as they are more disposed to listen to the councils of the wise and good, in preference to the flattery of knaves. Society cannot exist unless a controlling power upon the will and appetite be placed somewhere, and the less of it there is within, the more there must be without. It is ordained in the eternal constitution of things, that men of intemperate minds cannot be free. Their passions forge their fetters.[33]

Rapacity is one's capacity for "taking by force; plundering,"or greed, etc. (See rapacious.) Tyrants, thieves and robbers carry within themselves a high degree of rapacity. Knaves are "dishonest, deceitful" persons; tricky rascals or rogues etc. Temperate means to be "self-restrained," moderate "in one's actions, [and] speech," etc. Intemperate means to be "self-indulgent," thus an intemperate man acts generally to make himself feel good. A fetter is a "shackle or chain for the feet."[34]

If virtue does not moderate our actions or speech, and provide us with self-restraint, then what or who will? If virtue is necessary to bring order out of anarchy in a republic, then is goodness not also required to bring order out of confusion in our own personal lives? Is it not self-evident that greater goodness within ourselves, will not only make us happier persons, but more productive ones as well— more useful both to ourselves and others?

So our first task in building greater freedom is to add more goodness and subtract more badness from our own lives. In the process we will become not only better people, but better neighbors, better bosses or employees. We will become better parents, better sons and daughters, better brothers and sisters to one another. As the apostle Paul urged, we must, "overcome evil with good" (Rom. 12:21). As bad men become good, as good men become more virtuous, we rebuild the foundations of our free nation. If we reverse that direction, then we weaken those foundations. We also weaken the foundations of our own success. If you or I can add more goodness to our lives, it can only make us freer, happier and more prosperous, so this is the task I set before you.

To accomplish this task, I give you a book which was loved by our forefathers. It is the Bible. Our forefathers did not try to create their own virtue, nor did they try to separate goodness from either the Bible or religious faith. They studied the Bible and they prayed to God. No book has had more to say about good and evil, and so no book has been more important to our freedom. In a way, it is like a kind of Freedom Manual from God. It is effective only when we study it, refer to it, and apply it. This was the great key to the success of our Founding Fathers (as I will show later) and it will be the key to success in your own life.

Remember, George Washington believed: "It is impossible to rightly govern the world without God and the Bible."[35] James Madison described the great American adventure as a gamble, saying: "We have staked the whole future of American civilization, . . . upon the capacity of each and all of us to govern ourselves, to control ourselves, to sustain ourselves according to the Ten Commandments of God."[36] John Adams reiterated that republican government "is only to be supported by pure Religion or Austere Morals. Private, and public virtue is the only Foundation of Republics.[37] He also stressed: "Our Constitution was made only for a moral and religious people.[38] And Benjamin Franklin said it all. "He who shall introduce into public affairs the principles of primitive Christianity will change the face of the world."[39] Or to put it another way: "He who shall introduce into his personal affairs the principles of primitive Christianity will change his own life." Franklin assumed the change would bring freedom. So do I.

1. Beth Kassab, "Columbine was battle between good and evil," The Orlando Sentinel, July 15, 1999, A-5; emphasis mine.

2. Ibid., A-1.

3. C. S. Lewis, Rehabilitations and Other Essays, "Our English Syllabus" (London: Oxford University Press, 1939), 82-83; emphasis mine.

4. Zbigniew Brzezinski, Out of Control: Global Turmoil on the Eve of the 21st Century (New York: Collier Books, 1993), 3-18.

5. David B. Guralnik, Editor In Chief, Webster's New World Dictionary of the American Language, Second College Edition (Cleveland · New York: William Collins + World Publishing Co., Inc., 1974), 708

6. The Constitution of the United States of America (New York: Barnes & Noble, 1995), 113.

7. David Eltis, "Europeans and the Rise and Fall of African Slavery in the Americas: An Interpretation," American Historical Review, December 1993, 1400, cited in Race and Culture, 186.

8. Thomas Sowell, Race and Culture: A World View (New York: Basicbooks, 1994), 186.

9. Ibid.

10. M. Stanton Evans, The Theme is Freedom (Washington, D.C.:Regnery Publishing, Inc., 1994), 27.

11. Warren Bennis, On Becoming a Leader (Reading, Massachusetts: Addison-Wesley Publishing Company, Inc., 1989), 18; emphasis mine.

12. Barbara W. Tuchman, The March of Folly (New York: Alfred A. Knopf, 1984), 18.

13. Ibid.

14. Ibid., 19.

15. Richard Vetterli and Gary Bryner, In Search of the Republic: Public Virtue and the Roots of American Government (Totowa, New Jersey: Rowman & Littlefield, Publishers, 1987), 15.

16. Alexis de Tocqueville, Democracy in America (New York: Everyman's Library, 1994), Vol. I, Ch. XVII, 308; emphasis mine.

17. Ibid.

18. Ibid., 20.

19. Webster's New World Dictionary, Second College Edition, 1587.

20. Vetterli, 50; emphasis mine.

21. Henry Halley, Halley' Bible Handbook (Grand Rapids, MI: Zondervan, 1927, 1968), 18 cited in Barton, The Myth of Separation, 248.

22. Thomas Jefferson, Notes on the State of Virginia, ed., William Peden (Chapel Hill, N.C.: University of North Carolina Press, 1955), 164-165 cited in Vetterli, 2; emphasis mine.

23. James Madison, cited in David Barton, The Myth of Separation (Aledo, Texas: WallBuilder Press, 1993), 245-246. See also Harold K. Lane, Liberty! Cry Liberty! (Boston: Lamb and Lamb Tractarian Society, 1939), 32-33; emphasis mine.

24. Warren-Adams Letters (Boston, MA: Massachusetts Historical Society, 1917), Vol. I, 222 cited in Barton, The Myth of Separation, 247; emphasis mine.

25. John Adams, The Works of John Adams, Vol. IX, 229 cited in Barton, The Myth of Separation, 247; emphasis mine.

26. Benjamin Franklin, The Writing of Benjamin Franklin, Jared Sparks, ed. (Boston: Tappan, Whittemore and Mason, 1840), Vol. X, p. 297, April 17, 1787 cited in Barton, The Myth of Separation, 247; emphasis mine.

27. Marshall and Manuel, The Light and the Glory, p. 370, n. 10. Quoting from Charles E. Kistler, This Nation Under God (Boston: Richard G. Badger, The Gorham Press, 1924), 83 cited in The Myth of Separation, 249; emphasis mine.

28. Alexander Hamilton, The Federalist, Number 1; emphasis mine.

29. Samuel Adams cited in Rosalie J. Slater, Teaching and Learning America's Christian History (San Francisco: Foundation for American Christian Education, 1965), 250-251; emphasis mine.

30. Edward E. Whitacre Jr., President and Jere B. Ratcliffe, Chief Scout Executive "The Values of Scouting: 'To Be Continued' Scouting: A Family Magazine, Volume 87, No. 6, November-December 1999, 6; emphasis mine.

31. Boy Scout Handbook TENTH EDITION (Irving, Texas: Boy Scouts of America, 1990), 5; emphasis mine.

32. Webster's New Biographical dictionary (Springfield, Mass.: MERRIAM-WEBSTER INC., Publishers, 1988), 153.

33. Edmund Burke, The Works of Edmund Burke, Vol. 4 (Waltham, Mass.: Little, Brown, 1866), 51-52; emphasis mine. Quoted from In Search of the Republic, 1.

34. Webster's New World Dictionary, 1177, 779, 1464, 517.

35. Henry Halley, Halley' Bible Handbook (Grand Rapids, MI: Zondervan, 1927, 1968), 18 cited in Barton, The Myth of Separation, 248.

36. James Madison, cited in David Barton, The Myth of Separation (Aledo, Texas: WallBuilder Press, 1993), 245-246. See also Harold K. Lane, Liberty! Cry Liberty! (Boston: Lamb and Lamb Tractarian Society, 1939), 32-33; emphasis mine.

37. Warren-Adams Letters (Boston, MA: Massachusetts Historical Society, 1917), Vol. I, 222 cited in Barton, The Myth of Separation, 247; emphasis mine.

38. John Adams, The Works of John Adams, Vol. IX, 229 cited in Barton, The Myth of Separation, 247; emphasis mine.

39. Marshall and Manuel, The Light and the Glory, p. 370, n. 10. Quoting from Charles E. Kistler, This Nation Under God (Boston: Richard G. Badger, The Gorham Press, 1924), 83 cited in The Myth of Separation, 249; emphasis mine.

4

Into Every Hamlet

About a year ago I started reading a quote by Daniel Webster about the consequence of not spreading the word of the Bible and using its precepts. A few of the words and expressions are difficult because they are outdated but the message is clear and will definitely never be outdated.

Here is Daniel Webster's statement:

"If religious books are not widely circulated among the masses in this country, and the people do not become religious, I do not know what is to become of us as a nation. And the thought is one to cause solemn reflection on the part of every patriot and Christian. If truth be not diffused, error will be; if God and his word are not known and received, the devil and his works will gain the ascendancy; if the evangelical volume does not reach every hamlet, the pages of a corrupt and licentious literature will; if the power of the gospel is not felt through the length and breadth of the land, anarchy and misrule, degradation and misery, corruption and darkness, will reign without mitigation or end."

In fact, it has been about a hundred years since Mr. Webster made this statement and we can check him. We can see if he was right or wrong. We can even take a closer look at regions of the country or groups of people and see differences in quality of life between people who ignore the Bible or people who adhere to God's word.

We can see from people in the highest levels of government, business and entertainment down to children in grade school, the effects of a God-less society. What an erosion in values, morals, and ethics with the dismissal of prayer in schools in 1963. Recently, I read an exchange on the Internet. This followed the tragic killings at Columbine High School in Colorado.

"Dear God, where were you? How could you let this tragedy happen?"

Response from God: "I'm sorry, they won't let me into the schools anymore."

The following is a selected portion of a study presented in video format by a foundation named the WallBuilders. The title of the video is *America's Godly Heritage*.

The Change

On June 25, 1962, the Supreme Court made a ruling that would dramatically affect the way of life of 97% of Americans. In Engle v. Vitale, the following 22-word prayer, uttered in a public school, would change the course of history,... "Almighty God, we acknowledge our dependence upon thee. We beg thy blessings upon us, our parents, our teachers, and our country."

The Supreme Court ruled that this simple prayer was "Unconstitutional," and had violated the rights of a schoolchild. The Court ruled "that Biblical concepts could have a damaging psychological impact on schoolchildren."

The court further redefined "church" from "being a federally established denomination," to "any religious activity performed in public."

This ruling was made entirely without precedent. Unlike the 1892 ruling that stated 87 precedents, this ruling allowed the minority 3% of the population to dictate to the majority 97% of the population how and where they could worship. The Court seemingly ignored all precedents and history in ruling to strike down prayer in schools.

(Subsequent Supreme Court rulings further removed from public schools the Bible, visible displays of personal prayer, posting of the Ten Commandments, and even a nursery rhyme which, though it didn't contain any specific religious references, anyone listening might think it referred to God.)

The Result

After all of these rulings, what has happened to the United States since the unprecedented 1962 decision? The following stats will paint a chilling picture of what these rulings have produced.

Teen Pregnancies

- Prior to the 1962/63 rulings, the numbers held steady at about 13 per 1,000.
- Since 1962/63, the levels have risen steadily every year. Among the 10 to 14 year olds, the pregnancy rate has risen an incredible 553%!

STD's (Sexually Transmitted Diseases)

- Prior to 1962/63, new cases averaged about 400 per 100,000.
- Today, that number has increased 300% to 1,200 per 100,000.

Premarital Sex

- Among 16 year olds, up 365%.
- Among 17 year olds, up 271%.
- Among 18 year olds, up 208%.

Divorce
- Prior to 1962/63, about 1 in 12 couples got divorces.
- Today, about 4 in 7 marriages end in divorce.

Single Parent Families
- Up 140%.

Unmarried Couples
- Up 536%

Violent Crimes
- Since 1962/63, up a sobering 794%!

A Dubious Honor
The United States has become the world leader in
Violent Crimes;
Voluntary Abortions;
Illegal Drug Use;
and Illiteracy (among Industrialized nations).

Prior to 1962/63, every statistic listed above held a steady rate for decades. This next statistic is perhaps the most telling.

SAT's (The Scholastic Aptitude Test)
- Prior to 1962/63, there had never been more than a two-year period of a rise or decline of the scores. Again, everything held steady.
- Since 1692/63, SAT scores plummeted for 18 consecutive years. Currently, there is an 80-point difference between the scores prior to 1962/63, and today.

Private Schools

- Prior to 1962/63 there were 1,000 private/religious schools across the country.
- Today, there are over 32,000 private/religious schools, 8.5 million students attend these schools.

Public Schools

It is estimated that today's schools turn out 700,000 graduates every year that cannot even read their diploma.

The Supreme Court rulings of the 1960s, 70s, and early 80s have essentially changed the fabric of the First Amendment. The very Christian principles that established this country through prayer and inspiration, and which each of the Founding Fathers clearly acknowledged, have been thrown out, or ignored. Instead of going forth strong, and free, the citizens of the United States are seeing less and less of the real freedom our Founders dictated. Indeed, the minority few have forever changed the course upon which our Founding Fathers set this vessel called Democracy.

Have you noticed a lack of Bible usage and quotations in business and government life? Except for a few specialty books and magazines, there is truly a "famine in the land." Thanks to Forbes Magazine for their use of quotes and scriptures on their last page. The scriptural silence is deafening.

It's not that the Bible is just forgotten it has been forsaken. If your heart is right, the following will help. I want to do my part to bring these great words back into use.

I place these quotations here to help. My desire is to not just help you see the importance of the scriptures, but to inculcate a desire within you to read and use the scriptures within your family. The family is the place to build up our children. Is it any wonder that the adversary is working so hard to destroy the family? The battle for the hearts and souls of our children is real. Scriptures, prayer, and godly examples in leadership are our only weapons. God's word is sure and trustworthy.

Success American Style

It is impossible to mentally or socially enslave a Bible-reading people.

~Horace Greeley

Men and times change - but principles - never!

~Grover Cleveland

Of all the work that is done or that can be done for our country, the greatest is that of educating the body, the mind, and above all the character, giving spiritual and moral training to those who in a few years are themselves to decide the destinies of the nation.

~Theodore Roosevelt

Prayer includes praise and thanksgiving, intercession and petition, meditation, and confession. In prayer we focus fully on our God.

~Charles Swindoll

A feeling of real need is always a good enough reason to pray.

~Hannah Whitall Smith

The Church can have light only as it is full of the Spirit, and it can be full only as the members that compose it are filled individually.

~A. W. Tozer

We cannot produce revival, earn revival, or arrange God's timetable of revival visitation. We can only meet God's conditions and seek His face.

~Wesley Duewel

The Bible is the cornerstone of liberty.

~Thomas Jefferson

Into Every Hamlet

If you are sincerely willing to be restored, reshaped, refreshed and renewed by the Spirit of God, you will begin to discover a dimension of living you've never known before.

~Charles Swindoll

The law of the Lord is perfect, converting the soul: the testimony of the Lord is sure, making wise the simple. The statutes of the Lord are right, rejoicing the heart: the commandment of the Lord is pure, enlightening to the eyes.

~Psalms 19:7-8

In Christ, and through faith in him we may approach God with freedom and confidence.

~Ephesians 3:12 (NIV)

And he changeth the times and the seasons: he removeth kings and setteth up kings: he giveth wisdom unto the wise, and knowledge to them that know understanding.

~Daniel 2:21

The Lord will guide you always;

he will satisfy your needs in a sun-scorched land

and will strengthen your frame.

You will be like a well-watered garden,

like a spring whose waters never fail.

~Isaiah 58:11 (NIV)

Blessed is that man that maketh the Lord his trust...

~Psalm 40:4

God is our refuge and strength, a very present help in trouble.

~Psalm 46:1

Success American Style

Hold fast to the Bible as the . . .anchor of your liberties; write its precepts on your heart and practice them in your lives. To the influence of this Book, we are indebted for the progress made, and to this we must look as our guide in the future.

~Ulysses S. Grant

Remember them which have the rule over you, who have spoken unto you the word of God: whose faith follow, considering the end of their conversation. Jesus Christ the same yesterday, and today, and for ever.

~Hebrews 13:7-8

The Lord is nigh unto all them that call upon him, to all that call upon him in truth. He will fulfil the desire of them that fear him: he also will hear their cry, and will save them.

~Psalms 145:18-19

There is nothing but God's grace. We walk upon it; we breathe it; we live and die by it.

~Robert Louis Stevenson

Amazing Grace

Amazing Grace - how sweet the sound -
That saved a wretch like me!
I once was lost but now am found,
Was blind but now I see.
'Twas grace that taught my heart to fear,
and grace my fears relieved;
How precious did that grace appear
The hour I first believed!

~John Newton

A Christian man is the most free lord of all, and subject to none; a Christian man is the most dutiful servant of all, and subject to everyone.

~Martin Luther

Now, not only should the words of God be taught, pondered, and acted upon, but also we can take a new, more active look at how we can be a bigger part in God's cause.

I've quoted from II Peter 3:11 before, in the section on "being." This scripture also mentions that things will be dissolved. Then the question is asked, "...What manner of persons ought ye to be?" The question is more complete: "in all holy conversation and holiness?" Now to the far-reaching answer and challenge: "Looking for and hasting unto the coming of the day of God..." (verse 2)

Deeply embedded in Jewish scripture is the command to literally work to prepare and bring forth, indeed, to hasten the Lord's coming. "The day of the Lord" is spoken of frequently in the Tanakh (Jewish Bible or our Old Testament arranged differently). Examples can be located in Isaiah 13:9, 61:2; Jeremiah 46:10; Joel 1:15; Zephaniah 1:14-16; and Malachi 3:2, 3:23.

Many Christians (and Jews) are surprised to find the same challenge in the New Testament. Read with me Hebrews, Chapter 10:25. You will see that the challenge or command is that as the Day of the Lord grows near, we need to do more.

"Nor forsaking the assembling of ourselves together, as the manner of some it is; but exhorting one another; and so much the more, as ye see the day approaching."

And what is the alternative? To be lazy in these matters; to care not; to put off and procrastinate these works? It doesn't seem like a viable alternative because the results are horrible.

Success American Style

"Let us then be up and doing,
With a heart for any fate;
Still achieving, still pursuing,
Learn to labor and to wait."

~Last stanza of A Psalm of Life,
by Henry Wadsworth Longfellow)

I began this chapter with a quote from Daniel Webster, so let me turn to him again for a final fitting thought:

If we abide by the principles taught in the Bible, our country will go on prospering and to prosper; but if we and our posterity neglect its instructions and authority, no man can tell how sudden a catastrophe may overwhelm us and bury all our glory in profound obscurity.

~Daniel Webster

5
A Nation Undivided

Abraham Lincoln has always been one of my heroes. He is fascinating to me. I stand in awe of his thoughtful deliberations. He is truly one man who made a difference. I think we all know our country would have been torn asunder without him.

I attended Lincoln High School in Tacoma, Washington. For years we were the "Railsplitters," but about the time I graduated the team name changed to the "Abes." The Abes of Lincoln High School. I was proud to be an Abe.

Abraham Lincoln's message and pictures were everywhere. I stood in tears and disgust one morning when I saw that our rival high school had tarred and feathered Abe's statue. It took days to clean him up.

Well today, his messages do not need to be cleaned up. They are as powerful now as when written.

Battle Hymn of the Republic

Glory! Glory, hallelujah!
Glory! Glory, hallelujah!
Glory! Glory, hallelujah!
His truth is marching on.

Mine eyes have seen the glory of the coming of the Lord,
He is trampling out the vintage where the grapes of wrath are stored;
he hath loosed the fateful lightening of His terrible swift sword -
His truth is marching on.

I have seen him in the watch-fires of a hundred circling camps,
They have builded him an altar in the evening dews and damps;
I can read his righteous sentence by the dim and flaring lamps -
His day is marching on.

He has sounded forth the trumpet that shall never call retreat;
He is sifting out the hearts of men before his judgment-seat;
Oh, be swift, my soul, to answer him! be jubilant, my feet!
Our God is marching on.

In the beauty of the lilies Christ was born across the sea,
With a glory in his bosom that transfigures you and me;
As he died to make men holy, let us die to make men free,
While God is marching on.

~Julia Ward Howe

Regarding Abraham Lincoln

For three days in July 1863, Union and Confederate forces fought fierce battles at and near Gettysburg, Pennsylvania. The Union turned back one of the last major thrusts of the Confederate troops toward the North. Many consider it the turning point in the war; after Gettysburg, the South had to fight a defensive war that was doomed to fail.

In November of that same year, a battlefield cemetery was dedicated at Gettysburg. Edward Everett, a well-regarded and prominent speaker, was the main feature of the event. President Lincoln followed Everett's two hour speech with what came to be known as the Gettysburg Address. In about two minutes, Lincoln gave his speech; though the newspapers of the time had much to say about Everett's speech and relegated Lincoln to the back pages, Everett himself recognized the beauty of the simple elegance of Lincoln's words, and told the President as much in a note he wrote to him the next day.

The Gettysburg Address

"Four score and seven years ago our fathers brought forth on this continent a new nation, conceived in liberty and dedicated to the proposition that all men are created equal.

"Now we are engaged in a great civil war, testing whether that nation or any nation so conceived and so dedicated can long endure. We are met on a great battlefield of that war. We have come to dedicate a portion of that field as a final resting-place for those who here gave their lives that that nation might live. It is altogether fitting and proper that we should do this.

"But in a larger sense, we cannot dedicate, we cannot consecrate, we cannot hallow this ground. The brave men, living and dead who struggled here have consecrated it far above our poor power to add or detract. The world will little note nor long remember what we say here, but it can never forget what they did here. It is for us the living rather to be dedicated here to the unfinished work which they who fought here have thus far so nobly advanced. It is rather for us to be here dedicated to the great task remaining before us—that from these honored dead we take increased devotion to that cause for which they gave the last full measure of devotion—that we here highly resolve that these dead shall not have died in vain, that this nation under God shall have a new birth of freedom, and that government of the people, by the people, for the people shall not perish from the earth."

O Captain! My Captain!

O Captain! My Captain! our fearful trip is done,
The ship as weather'd every rack, the prize we sought is won
The port is near, the bells I hear, the people are exulting,
While follow eyes the steady keel, the vessel grim and daring;

But O heart! heart! heart!
O the bleeding drops of red,
Where on the deck my Captain lies,
Fallen cold and dead.

O Captain! My Captain! rise up and hear the bells;
Rise up-for you the flag is flung-for you the bugle trills,
For you bouquets and ribbon'd wreaths—for you the shores a-crowding,
For you they call—the swaying mass, their eager faces turning;

Here Captain!, dear father!
This arm beneath your head!
It is some dream that on the deck
You've fallen cold and dead.

My captain does not answer, his lips are pale and still,
My father does not feel my arm, he has no pulse nor will,
The ship is anchor'd safe and sound, its voyage closed and done,
From fearful trip the victor ship comes in with object won;

Exult O shores and ring O bells!
But I with mournful tread,
Walk the deck my captain lies,
Fallen cold and dead.

~Walt Whitman

6
Dare To Be Great

You, too, can achieve great things. The freedoms we enjoy provide fertile soil for achievement. There's an old proverb which says: "The biggest fish you'll ever catch is still swimming in the ocean." It's true.

With godly genes in our spiritual blood we are destined to greatness if only we will realize our potential, act on our inspiration and perform in right ways.

Truly, it can be said, that the only thing holding us back is our own drive or lack thereof.

I hope these thoughts help you see that you, too, can achieve whatever it is you want.

Lives of great men all remind us
We can make our lives sublime,
And, departing, leave behind us
Footprints on the sand of time;

Footprints, that perhaps another,
Sailing o'er life's solemn main,
A forlorn and shipwrecked brother,
Seeing, shall take heart again.

~Taken from a Psalm of Life
by Henry Wadsworth Longfellow

The following is an excerpt from a book by author Dr. Glenn I. Latham. If we turn our hearts to uplifting and inspiring our children, our nation will grow in ways that can't be measured. If you want to be truly great, be truly devoted to your children.

Dr. Latham's book can be found in better bookstores everywhere, or you can order a copy from Origin Book Sales at 1-888-467-4446.

Christlike Parenting

Parents can get so bogged down with parenting woes that they are often unable to imagine that things can get any better. Too often, if they lose hope, they won't even try. A vision of Christlike parenting helps us see beyond the moment; it helps us put the highs and lows of parenting into their proper perspective. It reminds us that today is not forever. With an overarching vision of His mission, Christ Himself saw beyond His suffering into eternity and received strength to finish His work.

Even a temporary departure from Christlike parenting can bring regret. The Reverend Billy Graham, in his autobiography, Just As I Am, acknowledged as one of his greatest regrets the time

he spent away from his children during their growing up years:
"Every day I was absent from my family is gone forever" (Briggs,
Graham Looks Back, B1)

When faced with a perplexing family dilemma, I find that the best hope for resolution is found in the answer to the question, "What would Jesus do?" His path was a straight path marked by perfect love and persuasion, by gentleness and meekness, by kindness, and pure knowledge. He was full of patience and long-suffering. If everyone would parent as Christ would parent, there would be no need for the hundreds of parenting books published over the years.

The teachings of Jesus Christ, used in concert with principles of behavioral science, can benefit parents immensely as they work to solve the problems of child-rearing. Following a talk I gave that placed this science in a Christian perspective, an appreciative mother wrote to me, "I am amazed at how well it works. I have peace at last in my family. Peace at last!" On the mud wall of the hut which Mahatma Gandhi called home hung but one adornment: a black and white picture of Jesus Christ with the inscription "He is our peace" (Fischer, 333). Regardless of your personal creed, being a Christlike parent will bring you peace.

Several reviewers of this manuscript expressed concern that the "suggestions and alternatives seem so natural and so perfect that they are almost unbelievable. The approach may seem too simple or even appear to be overly permissive for parents who have been inclined to use coercion."

Well, it is not easy, especially at first. It takes time and practice, as does learning any new skill. Whether learning to play the piano well, drive a car safely, or parent effectively, it takes time and practice. But it can be done, and the effort is worth it. Parents and teachers I work with do it all the time. The accounts of their successes would fill volumes far in excess of the number of pages in this book.

Shortly before this book went to press, a mother dropped by my office. I was leaving, she was entering, and we met at the door. She handed me a sheet of paper and said, "Here, I want you to know this." This is that letter, slightly edited to protect anonymity.

Success American Style

March 24, 1998

To Whom It May Concern:

One of our greatest blessings in life has been to come to know these principles. We have relied upon them as we have raised our seven children. It is amazing to me how such a few basic principles can apply to such a multiplicity of situations. They have helped us deal with tantrums, excessive fears, fights, bed wetting, broken rules, housework, homework, and hundreds of other situations. These principles work, and they work without screaming, coercion, physical violence, or anger. Best of all, behavior is changed with the self-esteem of the child intact.

I am especially grateful for these principles and how they have impacted our lives during the past year. Our 18-year-old son has suffered from Obsessive Compulsive Disorder (OCD) for the past 11 years, but we didn't realize what it was until one year ago. We just watched as our little boy became more and more withdrawn and sad. Each year of middle school and early high school became more of a challenge to him. It wasn't until he could no longer function in school and we felt we were on the verge of losing him that we contacted Dr. Latham again. We started a journey of treatment that has proven beyond any doubt that behavioral therapy administered in a Christlike way is one of the greatest tools we have in our society today, and it has the potential of being able to help solve many of our greatest problems. After only a few months on his program, life began to make sense to our son. He was able to overcome the obsessions and compulsions that had held him captive for so long. For the first time in years, he is a happy, well-adjusted young man who has gained thirty pounds, became an Eagle Scout, is eager to go to college and is anxious to help anyone who is suffering as he did. We have seen a miracle, and although his OCD may surface throughout his life, he now has the tools to help him through it.

These Christlike principles of behavior therapy work. They are proven, they are simple, and they can help build strong, happy, functioning individuals and families. Every relationship we have can be enriched through this Christlike way of dealing with God's children.

Beyond any doubt, I know that these principles are deeply anchored in eternal truths.

Though effective parenting is not necessarily easy, we typically make it a lot tougher than it should be. My wife and I were reminded of that in a stunning way during a recent weekend visit with friends of ours whom we hadn't seen in years. They have a family of seven children. Upon returning home, I made this entry in my journal:

As we visited in their humble little home, sparsely furnished, meager and scant in every way imaginable, I thought to myself, "Indeed, in our Father's House are many mansions, and this is one of them—one of the grander ones."

As parents, our friends do everything right. They pray together on bended knees. They watch TV together around the only TV set in the house—TV that is monitored and managed by the parents. They work together side-by-side. They eat together around the same table. They smile at and laugh with each other. The children play together, sharing the few toys they have. The parents tenderly hug and sweetly touch their children, and each other. They speak softly to their children. They read the scriptures together, and they help their neighbors. They worship together, and they turn their hearts and thoughts to God.

In the two days we spent with them, I saw more about how to properly parent than is contained in anything I, or any other author, ever wrote on the matter. Good parenting is not rocket science.

Yesterday and today I observed what was very probably the greatest lesson in effective parenting I ever witnessed, and it was delivered in a family presided over by a man I taught as a boy 36 years ago; a boy who, at the time, was classified as mildly mentally retarded.

When you think good parenting is so tough, give that some thought.

My hope is that this book will advance your progress toward becoming a Christlike parent, the only approach to parenting that can hope to be permanently right.

Glenn Latham

Success American Style

Because of what America is and what America has done, a firmer courage, a higher hope, inspires the heart of all humanity.

~Calvin Coolidge

Above all be of single aim; have a legitimate and useful purpose, and devote yourself unreservedly to it.

Don't let life discourage you; everyone who got where he is had to begin where he was.

~Richard L. Evans

I am not afraid of storms for I am learning to sail my ship.

~Louisa May Alcott

Show me a person who has never made a mistake and I'll show you somebody who has never achieved much.

~Joan Collins

There are no secrets to success. It is the result of perpetration, hard work, and learning from failure.

~General Colin Powell

If you want to be successful, it's just this simple: know what you're doing. Love what you're doing. And believe in what you're doing.

~Will Rogers

Leadership to me means duty, honor, country. It means character and it means listening from time to time.

~George Bush

Some men succeed because they are destined to, but most because they are determined to.

~Anonymous

Love what you do. Believe in your instincts. And you'd better be able to pick yourself up and brush yourself off every day. While life is not always fair, it is manageable. It is a matter of attitude and confidence.

~Mario Andretti

Opportunity knocks as often as a man has an ear trained to hear it, an eye trained to see it, a hand trained to grasp it, and a head trained to utilize it.

~Andrew Carnegie

Progress, or perish.

~B. H. Roberts

I do the very best I know how; the best I can; and I mean to keep doing so until the end. If the end brings me out all right, what is said against me won't amount to anything.

~Abraham Lincoln

Nothing is invented and perfected at the same time.

~John Ray

We shouldn't spend our lives solving little problems: we need to learn how to live with the little problems, and get on to bigger and better ones.

~David M. Kennedy

To accomplish great things we must no only act, but also dream; not only plan, but also believe.

~Anatole Frances

Happiness is a how, not a what; a talent, and not an object.

~Hermann Hesse

Success American Style

Many men owe the grandeur of their lives to their tremendous difficulties.

~Walter Spurgeon

Quitters never win. Winners never quit.

~Virginia Hutchinson

Follow through: stopping at third base adds no more to the score than striking out.

~Alexander Animator

If you are not afraid to face the music, you may get to lead the band some day.

~Edwin H. Stuart

The people who get on in this world are the people who get up and look for the circumstances they want; if they don't find them, they make them.

~George Bernard Shaw

Do not go where the path may lead. Go instead where there is no path, and blaze a trail.

~Anonymous

You cannot control the length of your life, but you can control its breadth, depth and height.

~Anonymous

Patience is a necessary ingredient of genius.

~Benjamin Disraeli

Indecision mars all success; there can be no good wind for the sailor who knows not to what port he is bound.

~Oliver Wendell Homes

If you wish success in life, make perseverance your bosom friend, experience your wise counselor, caution your elder brother, and hope your guardian genius.

~Joseph Addison

Have a purpose in life, and having it, throw into your work such strength of mind and muscle as God has given you.

~Thomas Carlyle

Not what men do worthily, but what they do successfully, is what history makes haste to record.

~Henry Ward Beecher

If you want to succeed in the world you must make your own opportunities as you go on. The man who waits for some seventh wave is a long time a coming. You can commit no greater folly then to sit by the roadside until some one comes along and invites you to ride with him to wealth or influence.

~John B. Gough

The quality of a man's life is in direct proportion to his commitment of excellence.

~Tom Landry

Cherish your visions and your dreams as they are the children of your soul; the blueprints of your ultimate achievements.

~Napoleon Hill

I do the very best I know how - the very best I can; and I mean to keep on doing it until the end.

~Abraham Lincoln

...be not afraid of greatness: some are born great, some achieve greatness, and some have greatness thrust upon them.

~William Shakespeare

Victory is not won in miles but in inches. Win a little now, hold your ground, and later win a little more.

~Louis L'Amour

My personal definition of success is - "peace of mind which is a direct result of self-satisfaction in knowing you made the effort to become the best of which you are capable." Failure to prepare is preparing to fail. Never try to be better than someone else, learn from others and never cease trying to be the best you can be.

~John R. Wooden

Take care of those who work for you and you'll float to greatness on their achievements.

~H. S. M. Burns

I often use a quote by Edward Everett Hale which best sums up my philosophy: "I am only one, but still I am one. I cannot do everything, but still I can do something. And because I cannot do everything, I will not refuse to do the something I can do. If everyone would take this to heart, most of our problems would be solved and there would be no need for organizations such as Mothers Against Drunk Driving.

~Candace Lightner, Founder,
Mothers Against Drunk Driving

No one can possibly achieve any real and lasting success or "get rich" in business by being a conformist.

~J. Paul Getty

The person who knows "how" will always have a job. The person who knows "why" will always be his boss.

~Diane Ravitch

One of the strongest characteristics of genius is the power of lighting its own fire.

~John Foster

Let us not dream that reason can ever be popular. Passions, emotions, may be made popular, but reason remains ever the property of the few.

~Goethe

God, who has given the Bible, has also given us our reason with which to examine and understand it; and we are guilty before him if we bury this talent in the earth and hide our Lord's money.

~J. F. Clarke

Never one thing and seldom one person can make for a success. It takes a number of them merging into one perfect whole.

~Marie Dressler

I honor any man who in the conscious discharge of his duty dares to stand alone.

~Charles Sumner

It gave me great joy to have some brothers come and tell about your faithfulness to the truth and how you continue to walk in the truth...Dear friend, you are faithful in what you are doing for the brothers, even though they are strangers to you.

~3 John 3,5 (NIV)

Humility is perfect quietness of heart. It is to have no trouble. It is never to be fretted or irritated or sore or disappointed. It is to expect nothing, to wonder at nothing that is done to me. It is to be at rest when nobody praises me and when I am blamed or despised. It is to have a blessed home in the Lord, where I can go in and shut the door and kneel to my Father in secret, and am at peace as in the deep sea of calmness when all around and above is trouble.

~Andrew Murray

Jesus himself has shown us by his own example that prayer and fasting are the first and most effective weapons against the forces of evil.

~Pope John Paul II

Love of prayer is one of the marks of the Spirit.

~Andrew Murray

Do not forsake wisdom, and she will protect you; love her, and she will watch over you. Wisdom is supreme; therefore get wisdom. Though it cost all you have, get understanding.

~Proverbs 4:6-7(NIV)

The Lord loves the just and will not forsake his faithful ones.

~Psalm 37:28 (NIV)

Examine me, O Lord, and prove me; try my reins and my heart. For thy lovingkindness is before mine eyes: and I have walked in thy truth.

~Psalm 26:2-3

The heart of the prudent getteth knowledge; and the ear of the wise seeketh knowledge

~Proverbs 18:15

Apply thin heart unto instruction, and thine ears to the words of knowledge.

~Proverbs 23:12

And whatsoever ye do, do it heartily, as to the Lord, and not unto men; knowing that of the Lord ye shall receive the reward of the inheritance: for ye serve the Lord Christ.

~Colossians 3:23-24

True repentance is to cease from sin.

~Saint Ambrose

...Deal courageously, and the Lord shall be with the good.

~2 Chronicles 19:11

Before there can be a fullness there must be emptiness. Before God can fill us with Himself we must first be emptied of our selves.

~A. W. Tozer

If God's people hunger deeply enough, God will hear and send revival. God requires more than casual prayers for revival. He wants His people to hunger and thirst for His mighty working. To seek God's face is far more than occasionally mentioning revival in our prayer. It involves repeated and prolonged prayer. It requires holy determination in prayer, examining ourselves to see if anything in our lives is hindering God.

~Wesley Duewel

Finally, brethren, whatsoever things are true, whatsoever things are honest, whatsoever things are just, whatsoever things are pure, whatsoever things are lovely, whatsoever things are of good report; if there be any virtue, and if there be any praise, think on these things.

~Philippians 4:8

Honor the Lord with your wealth.

~Proverbs 3:9 (NIV)

I hope I shall always possess firmness and virtue enough to maintain what I consider the most enviable of all titles, the character of an "Honest Man."

~George Washington

If you want to be respected for your actions, then your behavior must be above reproach. If our lives demonstrate that we are peaceful, humble, and trusted, this is recognized by others.

~Rosa Parks

Success American Style

Do you wish to be great? Then begin by being. Do you desire to construct a vast and lofty fabric? Think first about the foundations of humility. The higher your structure is to be, the deeper must be its foundation.

~St. Augustine

It is a great deal better to live a holy life than to talk about it. Lighthouses do not ring bells and fire cannons to call attention to their shining – they just shine.

~Dwight D. Moody

Peace, like charity, begins at home.

~Franklin D. Roosevelt

Humility like darkness reveals the heavenly lights.

~Henry David Thoreau

You gain strength, courage, and confidence by every experience in which you really stop to look fear in the face...you must do the thing you think you cannot do.

~Eleanor Roosevelt

...For unto whomsoever much is given, of him shall be much required: and to whom men have committed much, of him they will ask the more.

~Luke 12:48

An investment in knowledge always pays the best interest.

~Benjamin Franklin

The higher a man is in grace, the lower he will be in his own esteem.

~Charles Haddon Spurgeon

The Bible is the rock on which our republic rests.

~Andrew Jackson

The more profoundly we study this wonderful Book and the more closely we observe its divine precepts, the better citizens we will become and the higher will be the destiny of our nation.

~William McKinley

God's Word, contained in the Bible, has furnished all necessary rules to direct our conduct.

~Noah Webster

Wisdom is knowing when you can't be wise.

~Paul Engle

God gives us biblical principles not so that we can arrange our lives according to our taste, but so that we can know how God wants us to live.

~Larry Crabb

We are confronted with insurmountable opportunities.

~Pogo

He is most cheated who cheats himself.

~Leonard Drozd

In all things preserve integrity, and the consciousness of thine own uprightness will alleviate the toil of business, soften the hardness of ill-success and disappointment, and give thee an humble confidence before God when the ingratitude of men, or the iniquity of the items may rob thee of other reward.

~Paley

A straight line is the shortest in morals as in mathematics.

~Maria Edgeworth

A wise man will make more opportunities than he finds.

~Francis Bacon

Success American Style

Every human being is intended to have a character of his own; to be what no other is, and to do what no other can do.

~William Ellery Channing

Knowing is not enough; we must apply. Willing is not enough; we must do.

~Goethe

Develop the hunters attitude, the outlook that wherever you go, there are ideas waiting to be discovered.

~Roger Von Oech

Keep away from people who try to belittle your ambitions. Small people always do that, but the really great make you feel that you too can become great.

~Mark Twain

Chance favors the informed mind.

~Louis Pasteur

The highest possible reward for any man's toil is not what he gets for it, but what he becomes by it.

~John Ruskin

No abilities, however splendid, can command success without intense labor and persevering application.

~Alexander T. Stewart

Whatever the mind can conceive and believe, men can achieve.

~Andrew Carnegie

The secret of success in life, is for a man to be ready for his opportunity when it comes.

~Benjamin Disraeli

7
Documents Inspired By God

In the beginning of this book, I commented on people being led here by inspiration. I also believe the freedoms we enjoy and the written documents are gifts from God.

This chapter contains parts of two of our greatest documents. They have stood the test of time and these works should also be established in our hearts. We should know them so well as to quote from them.

These messages ring as true today as they did when written. They are our Declaration of Independence, the Preamble to our Constitution, and the first ten amendments to the Constitution, also known as the Bill of Rights.

Let's start with Christopher Columbus' statement about the inspiration he received in coming here.

Success American Style

O Lord, Almighty and everlasting God, by Thy Word Thou hast created the heaven, and the earth, and the sea; blessed and glorified be Thy Name, and praised be Thy Majesty, which hath deigned to use us, Thy humble servants, that Thy holy Name may be proclaimed in this second part of the earth.

~Christopher Columbus

Time passed. Then, as America struggled to become free, some of the greatest men ever to walk the earth raised their voices in defense of God and country. Patrick Henry was not the least of these. Just before the signing of the Declaration of Independence he talked of God. Note his comments:

"Yes, were my soul trembling on the wing of eternity, were this hand freezing to death, were my voice choking with the last struggle, I would still, with the last gasp of that voice, implore you to remember the truth. God has given America to be free."

Others who spoke in defense of America were John Adams, Alexander Hamilton, John Hancock, and Benjamin Harrison. As president of the United States, Thomas Jefferson added his voice in his belief of God and this country: "I have sworn upon the altar of God eternal hostility against every form of tyranny over the mind of man."

As the Constitution of the United States came into being, Benjamin Franklin gave his support to the deliberations of the representatives of the Colonies. Listen to these great words:

"I have lived a long time, and the longer I live, the more convincing proofs I see of this truth: that God governs in the affairs of men. And if a sparrow cannot fall to the ground without his notice, is it probable that an empire can rise without his aid?"

~*Light of Liberty*, by Paul H. Dunn.
Used with permission

Declaration of Independence

In Congress, July 4, 1776

The unanimous Declaration of the thirteen United States of America

When in the course of human events, it becomes necessary for one people to dissolve the political bands which have connected them with another, and to assume among the powers of the earth, the separate and equal station to which the Laws of Nature and of Nature's God entitle them, a decent respect to the opinions of mankind requires that they should declare the causes which impel them to the separation.

We hold these truths to be self-evident, that all men are created equal, that they are endowed by their Creator with certain unalienable Rights, that among these are Life, Liberty and the pursuit of Happiness. That to secure these rights, Governments are instituted among Men, deriving their just Powers from the consent of the governed, — That whenever any Form of Government becomes destructive of these ends, it is the Right of the People to alter or to abolish it, and to institute new Government, laying its foundation on such principles and organizing its powers in such form, as to them shall seem most likely to effect their Safety and Happiness. Prudence, indeed, will dictate that Governments long established should not be changed for light and transient causes; and accordingly all experience hath shewn, that mankind are more disposed to suffer, while evils are sufferable, than to right themselves by abolishing the forms to which they are accustomed. But when a long train of abuses and usurpations, pursuing invariably the same Object evinces a design to reduce them under absolute Despotism, it is their right, it is their duty, to throw off such Government, and to provide new guards for their future security — Such has been the patient sufferance of these Colonies; and such is now the necessity which constrains them to alter their former Systems of Government. — The history of the present King of Great Britain is a history of repeated injuries and usurpations, all having in direct object the establishment of an absolute Tyranny over these States. To prove this, let facts be submitted to a candid world.

He has refused his Assent to Laws, the most wholesome and necessary for the public good.

He has forbidden his Governors to pass Laws of immediate and pressing importance, unless suspended in their operation till his Assent should be obtained; and when so suspended, he has utterly neglected to attend to them.

He has refused to pass other Laws for the accommodation of large districts of people, unless those people would relinquish the right of Representation in the Legislature, a right inestimable to them and formidable to tyrants only.

He has called together legislative bodies at places unusual, uncomfortable, and distant from the depository of their Public Records, for the sole purpose of fatiguing them into compliance with his measures.

He has dissolved Representative Houses repeatedly, for opposing with manly firmness his invasions on the rights of the people.

He has refused for a long time, after such dissolutions, to cause others to be elected; whereby the Legislative Powers, incapable of Annihilation, have returned to the People at large for their exercise; the State remaining in the mean time exposed to all the dangers of invasion from without, and convulsions within.

He has endeavoured to prevent the population of these States; for that purpose obstructing the Laws for Naturalization of Foreigners; refusing to pass others to encourage their migrations hither, and raising the conditions of new Appropriations of Lands.

He has obstructed the Administration of Justice, by refusing his Assent to Laws for establishing Judiciary Powers.

He has made Judges dependent on his Will alone, for the tenure of their offices, and the amount and payment of their salaries.

He has erected a multitude of New Offices, and sent hither swarms of Officers to harrass our People, and eat out their substance.

He has kept among us, in times of peace, Standing Armies without the Consent of our legislatures.

He has affected to render the Military independent of and superior to the Civil Power.

He has combined with others to subject us to a jurisdiction foreign to our constitution, and unacknowledged by our laws; giving his Assent to their Acts of pretended Legislation:

For Quartering large bodies of armed troops among us:

For protecting them, by a mock Trial, from Punishment for any Murders which they should commit on the Inhabitants of these States:

For cutting off our Trade with all parts of the world:

For imposing Taxes on us without our Consent:

For depriving us in many cases, of the benefits of Trial by Jury:

For transporting us beyond seas to be tried for pretended offences:

For abolishing the free system of English Laws in a neighbouring Province, establishing therein an Arbitrary government, and enlarging its Boundaries so as to render it at once an example and fit instrument for introducing the same absolute rule into these Colonies:

For taking away our Charters, abolishing our most valuable Laws, and altering fundamentally the forms of our Governments:

For suspending our own Legislature, and declaring themselves invested with power to legislate for us in all cases whatsoever.

He has abdicated Government here, by declaring us out of his Protection and waging War against us.

He has plundered our seas, ravaged our Coasts, burnt our towns, and destroyed the lives of our people.

He is at this time transporting large Armies of foreign Mercenaries to compleat the works of death, desolation and tyranny, already begun with circumstances of Cruelty and perfidy scarcely paralleled in the most barbarous ages, and totally unworthy the Head of a civilized nation.

He has constrained our fellow Citizens taken Captive on the high Seas to bear Arms against their Country, to become the executioners of their friends and Brethren, or to fall themselves by their Hands.

He has excited domestic insurrections amongst us, and has endeavoured to bring on the inhabitants of our frontiers, the merciless Indian Savages, whose known rule of warfare, is an undistinguished destruction of all ages, sexes and conditions.

In every stage of these Oppressions we have Petitioned for Redress in the most humble terms: Our repeated Petitions have been answered only by repeated injury. A Prince, whose character is thus marked by every act which may define a Tyrant, is unfit to be the ruler of a free people.

Nor have we been wanting in attention to our Brittish brethren. We have warned them from time to time of attempts by their legislature to extend an unwarrantable jurisdiction over us. We have reminded them of the circumstances of our emigration and settlement here. We have appealed to their native justice and magnanimity, and we have conjured them by the ties of our common kindred to disavow these usurpations, which, would inevitably interrupt our connections and correspondence. They too have been deaf to the voice of justice and of consanguinity. We must, therefore, acquiesce in the necessity, which denounces our Separation, and hold them, as we hold the rest of mankind, Enemies in War, in Peace Friends.

We, therefore, the Representatives of the United States of America, in General Congress, Assembled, appealing to the Supreme Judge of the world for the rectitude of our intentions, do, in the Name, and by Authority of the good People of these Colonies, solemnly publish and declare, That these United Colonies are, and of Right ought to be Free and Independent States; that they are absolved from all Allegiance to the British Crown, and that all political connection between them and the State of Great Britain, is and ought to be totally dissolved; and that as Free and Independent States, they have full Power to levy War, conclude Peace, contract Alliances, establish Commerce, and to do all other Acts and Things which Independent States may of right do.

And for the support of this Declaration, with a firm reliance on the protection of Divine Providence, we mutually pledge to each other our Lives, our Fortunes and our sacred Honor.

Signers of the Declaration of Independence

𝔓reamble to the Constitution

𝔚e the 𝔓eople of the 𝔘nited 𝔖tates, in 𝔒rder to form a more perfect 𝔘nion, establish 𝔍ustice, insure domestic 𝔗ranquility, provide for the common defense, promote the general 𝔚elfare, and secure the 𝔅lessings of 𝔏iberty to ourselves and our 𝔓osterity, do ordain and establish this Constitution for the 𝔘nited 𝔖tates of America.

Bill of Rights

Amendment I

Congress shall make no law respecting an establishment of religion, or prohibiting the free exercise thereof; or abridging the freedom of speech, or of the press; or the right of the people peaceably to assemble, and to petition the Government for a redress of grievances.

Amendment II

A well regulated Militia, being necessary to the security of a free State, the right of the people to keep and bear Arms, shall not be infringed.

Amendment III

No Soldier shall, in time of peace be quartered in any house, without the consent of the Owner, nor in time of war, but in a manner to be prescribed by law.

Amendment IV

The right of the people to be secure in their persons, houses, papers, and effects, against unreasonable searches and seizures, shall not be violated, and no Warrants shall issue, but upon probable cause, supported by Oath or affirmation, and particularly describing the place to be searched, and the persons or things to be seized.

Amendment V

No person shall be held to answer for a capital, or otherwise infamous crime, unless on a presentment or indictment of a Grand Jury, except in cases arising in the land or naval forces, or in the Militia, when in actual service in time of War or public danger; nor shall any person be subject for the same offense to be twice put in jeopardy of life or limb; nor shall be compelled in any criminal case to be a witness against himself, nor be deprived of life, liberty, or property, without due process of law; nor shall private property be taken for public use, without just compensation.

Amendment VI

In all criminal prosecutions, the accused shall enjoy the right to a speedy and public trial, by an impartial jury of the State and district wherein the crime shall have been committed, which district shall have been previously ascertained by law, and to be informed of the nature and cause of the accusation; to be confronted with the witnesses against him; to have compulsory process for obtaining witnesses in his favor, and to have the Assistance of Counsel for his defence.

Amendment VII

In Suits at common law, where the value in controversy shall exceed twenty dollars, the right of trial by jury shall be preserved, and no fact tried by a jury, shall be otherwise re-examined in any Court of the United States, than according to the rules of the common law.

Amendment VIII

Excessive bail shall not be required, nor excessive fines imposed, nor cruel and unusual punishments inflicted.

Amendment IX

The enumeration in the Constitution, of certain rights, shall not be construed to deny or disparage others retained by the people.

Success American Style

Amendment X

The powers not delegated to the United States by the Constitution, nor prohibited by it to the States, are reserved to the States respectively, or to the people.

8

Honoring Those Who Served

They call it Christmas circle. It's a roundabout on the only corner which could possible require a traffic light in the small desert community of Borrego Springs, California. The traffic enters and goes counter clockwise and leaves one quarter, one-half or three quarters of the way around. Oh, and for fun you could go round and round.

My wife was raised there. It's so relaxing that after even just a few days I'm up early and ready to go. That is how I found myself one sunny Memorial Day morning. I went for a ride. I came through town and saw a few people gathering in the center of the circle. They were getting ready to raise the flag. A few veterans of WWII were there, now much older. I stopped to watch.

The music filled me and I had to work hard to hold back the tears. Usually my spiritual experiences have music as a part. Again, the music caused a major lump in my throat. These men were so proud of our country. They had risked their lives.

Success American Style

I too, am a veteran, but I served in no wars. My life was not at risk. I did not have to put it all on the line. Nevertheless, I sure appreciate those who did. I know thousands of Americans feel the same way. In a very small way I will dedicate the words of this chapter to the men and women who have served, fought, and died for our country to preserve the freedoms we enjoy.

I shall have no motive to influence my conduct in administering the Government except the desire ably and faithfully to serve my country and live in grateful memory of my countrymen.

~James Buchanan

Once again I'll liberally borrow from Paul Dunn the words out of the prologue of his book *The Light of Liberty.*

Prologue

It seems ironic that, as an eleventh-grade student at Hollywood High School in California, I was asked by my history teacher to prepare a report on a current event to give before the class. My subject was the fall of Bataan and Corregidor in December of 1941. Little did I realize as I stood before my class reporting General Douglas MacArthur's now-famous promise to the Philippine people, "I shall return," that I would be in the infantry assault wave on the island of Leyte on an October morning in 1944, two days ahead of that return.

Many years later, in General MacArthur's final address to the Corps of Cadets at West Point, he asked these would-be soldiers to remember throughout their careers and lives their motto of Duty, Honor, Country, which motto he and his comrades of three wars had held to while "bending under soggy packs, on many a weary march from dripping dusk to drizzling dawn, slogging ankle-deep through the mire of shell-shocked roads, to form grimly for the attack, blue-lipped, covered with sludge and mud, chilled by the wind and rain, driving home to their objective." He recalled "the filth of murky fox-holes, the stench of ghostly trenches, the slime of dripping dugouts; those broiling suns of relentless heat, those torrential rains of devastating storm, the loneliness and utter desolation of jungle trails, the bitterness of long separation from those they loved and cherished, and [the] deadly pestilence of tropical disease, the horror of stricken areas of war; their resolute and determined defense, their swift and sure attack, their indomitable purpose, their complete and decisive victory-always victory-always through the bloody haze of their last reverberating shot, the vision of gaunt, ghastly men reverently following [the] password of Duty-Honor-Country."

He concluded by saying that "the soldier, above all other people, prays for peace, for he must suffer and bear the deepest wounds and scars of war."[1]

To the thousands of patriots in our history who have known war firsthand and have experienced the price of liberty and peace, and to the tens of thousands like them who have followed, we, the current and future generations, owe tremendous gratitude and a continuing remembrance of the courage, devotion, and sacrifice that made America great.

I shall never forget the feelings I had as a young soldier when time after time I was called upon to place in shallow, temporary graves the lifeless bodies of my comrades in arms, some unknown to me, many others with whom I had trained and to whom I had grown close. I couldn't help but remember their wishes and desires for the future.

On an island far away in the Pacific, our regiment placed the following inscription above the entrance of a temporary cemetery:

We Gave Our Todays
In Order That You Might Have Your Tomorrows

May God grant us the vision, understanding, and determination to make those tomorrows worthy of the sacrifices of our hero dead, and may the world never forget that all future wars and conflicts will again and always cost the lives of the elite of our nations in order to keep the "light of liberty."

Success American Style

As Americans, we go forward, in the service of our country, by the will of God.

~Franklin D. Roosevelt

Is life so dear, or peace so sweet, as to be purchased at the price of chains and slavery? Forbid it, Almighty God! I know not what course others may take but as for me; give me liberty or give me death.

~Patrick Henry

I therefore believe it is my duty to my Country to love it; to support its Constitution; to obey its laws; to respect its flag, and to defend it against all enemies.

~William Tyler Page

My prayer is that God will grant each one of us today a new beginning. With all my heart, I pray that every single one of us will determine, right now, in this hour, that we will stand firm, that we will join the mighty arm of the Lord, outfitted with spiritual armor, fully prepared to engage in the battle for the soul of America. And to overcome the world for Christ.

~James Kennedy

The power in the dream God dreams for you is stronger than the weight of tradition, mightier than the force of history. The right kind of dream can liberate an entire nation or emancipate a life from any negative circumstances.

~Wintley Phipps

Would you have peace with God?...the Lord Jesus has shed his heart's blood for this. He died for this; he rose again for this; he ascended into the highest heaven, and is now interceding at the right hand of God.

~George Whitefield

My Country, 'Tis of Thee

My country, 'tis of Thee,
Sweet land of liberty
Of thee I sing;
Land where my fathers died,
Land of the pilgrim's pride,
From every mountain side
Let freedom ring.

Our fathers' God to Thee,
Author of liberty,
To Thee we sing;
Long may our land be bright
With freedom's holy light;
Protect us by Thy might,
Great God our King.

~Samuel Francis Smith

Greater love has no one than this, that he lay down his life for his friends.

~John 15:13

So nigh is grandeur to our dust,
So near is God to man,
When Duty whispers low, "Thou must,"
The youth replies, "I can."

~Ralph Waldo Emerson

Our Flag: A Symbol of Service

June 14, 1777, the Continental Congress passed the first Flag Act: "Resolved, That the flag of the United States be made of thirteen stripes, alternate red and white; that the union be thirteen stars, white in a blue field, representing a new Constellation."

Act of April 4, 1818, provided for thirteen stripes - representing the thirteen original colonies, and one star for each state, to be added to the flag on the Fourth of July following the admission of each new state, signed by President Monroe.

Fear thou not; for I am with thee: be not dismayed; for I am thy God: I will strengthen thee; yea, I will help thee; yea, I will uphold thee with the right hand of my righteousness.

~Isaiah 41:10

Onward Christian Soldiers

Onward, Christian soldiers,
Marching as to war,
With the Cross of Jesus
Going on before.
Christ the royal Master
Leads against the foe;
Forward into battle,
See, his banners go!
Onward, Christian soldiers,
Marching as to war,
With the Cross of Jesus
Going on before.

At the sign of triumph
Satan's legions flee;
On then, Christian soldiers,
On to victory.

Hell's foundations quiver
At the shout of praise;
Brothers, lift your voices,
Loud your anthems raise.

Like a mighty army
Moves the Church of God;
Brothers, we are treading
Where the Saints have trod;
We are not divided,
All one body we,
One in hope and doctrine
One in charity:

Crowns and thorns may perish,
Kingdoms rise and wane,
But the Church of Jesus
Constant will remain;
Gates of hell can never
'Gainst that Church prevail;
We have Christ's own promise,
And that cannot fail.

Onward, then, ye people,
Join our happy throng,
Blend with ours your voices
In the triumph song;
Glory, laud and honour
Unto Christ the King;
This through countless ages
Men and Angels sing.
Onward, Christian soldiers,
Marching as to war,
With the Cross of Jesus
Going on before.

~Sabine Baring Gould

Success American Style

Service is the supreme commitment of life.

~Warren G. Harding

My goodness, and my fortress; my high tower, and my deliverer; my shield, and he in whom I trust; who subdueth my people under me.

~Psalms 144:2

Be alert to give service. What counts a great deal in life is what we do for others.

~Anonymous

Paul H. Dunn, my friend, passed away in 1997. His friend, Senator Orrin Hatch, wrote these words to a very beautiful and melodic song for his funeral. I wish to honor Paul Dunn here for a lifetime of service to God, to his fellow man, and to his wife and family.

It was a distinct pleasure to know him and hear is counsel.

This Good Man

(Especially for Elder Paul H. Dunn)

This good man who humbly taught
Love of heaven, love of God,
Fixed his heart on things above,
Teaching men with words of love
He who truly loved the Lord
Led many to His word.

This good man so tenderly,
Loved his family,
Guiding, leading each dear one
Back to one celestial home
He who walked the narrow way,
Prepared his family.

This good man of destiny
Loved his country zealously;
Testified that this great land
Drew its pow'r from God's own hand.
He who loved and feared his God
Stood tall in freedom's cause.

Like Paul of old he suffered thorns
Earthly trials and daunting storms,
But earnestly he sought the Lord,
Humbly earning his reward.

This good man of royal birth,
Loved the things of greatest worth.
Hon'ring well his fellow man,
Fam'ly and his native land
Now his time on earth is done.
Eternal vic'try won!

9
Light Of Liberty

Our values, our principles, and our determination to succeed as a free and democratic people will give us a torch to light the way. And we will survive and become the stronger - not only because of patriotism that stands for love of country, but a patriotism that stands for love of people.

~Gerald Ford

For years I had been a big fan of Paul Dunn. Mr. Dunn was one of the most inspirational speakers I had ever heard. And prolific. He had written over 30 books and millions had been sold.

There I was, sitting beside him in the big seminar room at our corporate headquarters in Seattle. We were waiting for the flag. Once in the room, all arose to say the Pledge of Allegiance. He could barely get the words out. His eyes and cheeks were wet with tears.

Here was a man who had put his life in harms way for the country he loved. His love, undaunted, deeply affected me that day. He rose to speak and for several minutes disregarded his proposed text and shared insights about war, service, and patriotism. Everyone was affected and developed a better understanding of the greatness of our country and the people who have fought and died for our land. Here are his thoughts, in a slightly edited version:

Developing Uncommon People

by Paul H. Dunn

I had the opportunity of serving my country in the Pacific in 5 campaigns. Previously, I was interested in what they were teaching my grandson. So I started to read. There (were) two paragraphs taking us from the battle of Guam to the battle of Okinawa in the Pacific. That bothered me. I was in the initial landing at Guam in 1944 and I concluded my activity in the Pacific on the island of Okinawa in April of 1945. Okinawa is an island which is to Japan what Hawaii is to the US. It's a very wonderful luxurious island and it's a resort area. We landed there on Easter morning 1945. Okinawa happens to be the Easter lily capital of the world. I thought that was rather ironic. In 90 days, three months, 300,000 people died on that island, and you can drive around it in a couple of hours. That was civilians, soldiers on both sides, and even little children.

As I experienced that campaign, I helped lay several of my friends, also 19 and 20 year olds, in shallow graves. I don't mean to be depressing, but when a soldier is killed in a war, you have to do some rather crude things; One of which is to be sure you keep the body properly identified. A soldier always wears two dog tags, one of the dog tags you place in the mouth of the dead person, for as you place him in a grave, it may be several years before you can dig it up again, and the skull will have the proper identification of the dog tag. The other goes to the chaplain, in terms of registration of the dead.

On Okinawa, I was in the 77th Infantry Division. We lost several thousand young men, and I knew quite a few of them. You wrap them in a poncho and then take a bulldozer... and dig (a trench) about six feet deep and then place little individual graves for each soldier and bulldoze it back. That becomes a temporary cemetery for the soldiers until the war is completed or until they go back to recover. We did that many, many times and it's tender to place one of your friends in one of those shallow graves, who like you and me wanted to live and to have all the opportunities.

I was drafted in the first 18 year old ruling in WWII and didn't want to fight. I wanted to be a ball player, I wanted to have the good things in life. My goal was chasing girls and getting a car and having fun. And here the Army said, "No, you go out and kill some people you don't even know." Which I had to do in order to defend the freedom of this country, and I had to take many, many lives which I didn't even...people I didn't even know.

The cemetery on Okinawa for the 77th division, is what I thought about, as you were singing, I watched this flag. So when I pledge allegiance to that flag, I think about people that I served with who willingly laid down their life for this country, and I remember to enjoy the things that you and I enjoy today in a marvelous manner.

Paul Dunn passed away a few years ago. We miss him. His contribution goes on in written and spoken formats.

Paul H. Dunn's book *Light of Liberty* is passionate and dynamic. Every family should have it. In addition, his two great books *Success Formulas* and *Meaningful Living* are now reprinted. Call 1-888-467-4446 for information or to order a copy of an interview between Wade Cook and Janet Gough, Paul Dunn's oldest daughter.

Providing for the free exercise of religion is not just a constitutional mandate; it is a complex and demanding responsibility.

~William Dendinger

Freedom is one of the deepest and noblest aspirations of the human spirit.

~Ronald Reagan

Success American Style

For more than three centuries, moral values have been the life-support system of this country. The men and women who planted their stand on these shores in the year 1607 vowed to build here a nation founded on virtue and moral integrity. And during all those years their promises and plan held true. The American people brought forth on this continent a nation dedicated to liberty and justice. The founders were committed to strong moral principles based on individual liberty and personal responsibility.

~James Kennedy

We identify the flag with almost everything we hold dear on earth. It represents our peace and security, our civil and political liberty, our freedom of religious worship, our family, our friends, our home. We see it in the great multitude of blessings, of rights and privileges that make up our great country.

But when we look at our flag and behold it emblazoned with all our rights, we must remember that it is equally a symbol of our duties. Every glory that we associate with it is the result of duty done. A yearly contemplation of our flag strengthens and purifies the national conscience.

~Calvin Coolidge

Above all, we must realize that no arsenal, or no weapon in the arsenals of the world, is so formidable as the will and moral courage of free men and women.

~Ronald Reagan

We know what works: Freedom works. We know what's right: Freedom is right.

~George Bush

Freedom of religion, freedom of the press, and freedom of person under the protection of the habeas corpus, these are the principles that guided our steps through an age of revolution and reformation.

~Thomas Jefferson

Our God, we acknowledge that you are the Lord of the nations; that kingdoms, kings and queens, and political leaders rise and fall within the purpose and plan that you have for this universe. We thank you for the freedoms that we enjoy as part of this experiment in democracy that we call the United States. We thank you for the freedom of religion; that we can gather to sing of your faithfulness, to give of our resources, to open your Word, to listen to your voice; and we do it without harassment, intimidation, threat of imprisonment, or persecution.

~Edward Dobson

But I say to all men, what we have achieved in liberty, we will surpass in greater liberty. Steadfast in our faith in the Almighty, we will advance toward a world where man's freedom is secure.

~Harry S. Truman

Under the eternal urge of freedom we became an independent nation.

~Calvin Coolidge

Freedom of religion is written into the constitution. No state in the world has been so strongly influenced by biblical Christianity.

~Operation World

Freedom and the dignity of the individual have been more available and assured here than in any other place on Earth.

~Ronald Reagan

God grants liberty only to those who love it, and are always ready to guard and defend it.

~Daniel Webster

Posterity – you will never know how much it has cost my generation to preserve your freedom. I hope you will make good use of it.

~John Quincy Adams

Events have brought our American democracy to new influence and new responsibilities. They will test our courage, our devotion to duty, and our concept of liberty.

~Harry S. Truman

My fellow Americans: ask not what your country can do for you – ask what you can do for your country. My fellow citizens of the world: ask not what America will do for you, but what together we can do for the freedom of man.

~John F. Kennedy

In the beginning the Old World scoffed at our experiment; today our foundations of political and social belief stand unshaken, a precious inheritance to ourselves, an inspiring example of freedom and civilization to all mankind.

~Warren G. Harding

Under this covenant of justice, liberty, and union we have become a nation – prosperous, great, and mighty.

~Lyndon Baines Johnson

Proclaim liberty throghout all the land unto all the inhabitants thereof.

~Inscribed on Liberty Bell, Philadelphia, Pennsylvania

Under this Constitution the boundaries of freedom have been enlarged, the foundations of order and peace have been strengthened, and the growth of our people in all the better elements of national life has indicated the wisdom of the founders and given new hope to their descendants.

~James Garfield

A union depending not upon the constraint of force, but upon the loving devotion of a free people; "and that all things may be so ordered and settled upon the best and surest foundations that peace and happiness, truth and justice, religion and piety, may be established among us for all generations."

~Rutherford B. Hayes

Every subject's duty is the king's; but every subject's soul is his own.

~William Shakespeare

Liberty cannot be preserved without the general knowledge among the people.

~John Adams

It is an axiom in my mind that our liberty can never be safe but in the hands of the people themselves, and that, too, of the people with a certain degree of instruction.

~Thomas Jefferson

We cannot overestimate the fervent love of liberty, the intelligent courage, and the sum of common sense with which our fathers made the great experiment of self-government.

~James A. Garfield

Man is really free only in God, the source of his freedom.

~Sherwood Eddy

Freedom is one of the deepest and noblest aspirations of the human spirit.

~Ronald Reagan

He that is down, needs fear no fall;
He that is low, no pride;
He that is humble ever shall
Have God to be his guide.

~John Bunyan

I am a most unworthy sinner, but I have cried out to the Lord for grace and mercy, and they have covered me completely.

~Christopher Columbus

We've borrowed extensively from Paul H. Dunn, let us also conclude this chapter with his words:

"I conclude with the words of a well-known hymn of praise.

Our fathers' God, to thee,
Author of liberty,
To thee we sing;
Long may our land be bright
With freedom's holy light.
Protect us by thy might,
Great God, our King!

May that prayer be answered upon this great land because of our righteousness as individuals and as a nation."

10
To Be

I've long been fascinated by the verb "to be." I wrote about this very thing in *Don't Set Goals*. I submit that the typical goal setting method was inadequate. If you want to achieve something "be" rather than "try." Be that kind of person.

The be-attitudes are wonderful characteristics. They don't say "work at," or "try," or even "set a goal" to be pure in heart. In the Hebrew language there is not past nor future tense conjugation of this verb. It is all now. *I am* is a complete statement. It signifies past, present, and future. *I am* is the essence of life. *I am* is the word God used for Himself. "I am" as stated by Jesus is ultimately what led to his crucifixion.

The Apostle Peter asked, "What manner of person ought ye to be?" (II Peter 3:11) Christ says, "Be yea therefore perfect..." (Matthew 5:48). There is a lot more to this simple word than meets the eye.

Presented here are words of strength; messages of optimism; lessons in character; in short a promise to help us be all that we can be without joining the army.

I am confident God has so much in store for us that we can ever fathom. He knows us our strengths and weaknesses; our desires and needs. He will be true to us, even if we come up short. His promises are sure. In all this we need to find ourself-our true self. As you read the following words ask yourself this powerful and for reading question: "What is my mission for God and how will I be today?"

Our daughter, Leslie, loves horses. She would rather be with her horse than eat. My wife and other daughters, Carrie and Rachel, also love horses. They are very talented, and we go to a lot of horse shows. They ride (English style) and show at Halter, and Leslie even jumps and goes on fox hunts.

Leslie expressed a desire to compete at the Youth National Arabian Horse Show in Oklahoma City. There, that's the target. Thousands of kids want to go, a few hundred actually do. If you want to call this a goal, then fine, but let's explore how it happens. By the way, at the time I wrote this, Leslie and the horse qualified to go. We're packing our bags.

The large overriding question is this, "Are you willing to pay the price?"

There were several things to discuss, but remember, the price to pay is the most important.

Question: What do you have to do to get ready?

Answer: Practice, train the horse, enter it in a qualifying regional show, and place first or second.

Question: How do you get first or second?

Answer: Buy a quality horse and practice many hours. Practice perfect moves.

Question: When do you have to do this?

Answer: In a timely manner to qualify for the big show. Also, each show (regional) has entry deadlines.

Question: What price is necessary?

Answer:

1. Any of several hours or days to train, groom, and study.
2. Miss out on activities with friends.
3. Have sore muscles, et cetera.
4. Be gone from home.
5. Entry fees and training money (Mom and Dad pay this).

Then I threw in a negative. You know Oklahoma is mighty hot in July. "I don't care Dad, I want to go."

Now that we have discussed these things, we're ready to get on with it. To be a champion you must do what champions do.

Many of the youth who attended Nationals were featured in the *Arabian Horse Times* prior to the show. What follows are Leslie's comments from the magazine article:

NAME: Leslie Cook

FARM AFFILIATION: Amethyst Arabians

TRAINER & DIVISION(S): Mike Lamb/River Ridge Farm - Half-Arabian Country, Saddle Seat Equitation 14-17 and Arabian Mare Halter JOTH.

YEARS COMPETING: Two years.

MOST LOOKING FORWARD TO AT YOUTH NATIONALS: At every large and competitive horse show, I look forward to the thrill of it all. I love the feeling just knowing I'm at Nationals with great horses. I love the joy I feel inside knowing I did well, and dreaming of what's ahead for the future.

WHOM DO YOU MOST ADMIRE: The "horse show world" consists of a lot of people I admire and look up to. I admire anyone I see who has set high goals. And then, through hard work and determination, achieve their dream. I mostly admire my trainer, Mike. He is a great person and a true horseman. I love riding under his instruction because he builds confidence and self-esteem so I know I can achieve anything I set my heart on.

Success American Style

MOST IMPORTANT LESSON LEARNED: Though many, the most important lesson I have learned is to never let go of your dream. Work hard, harder, and your hardest and dedicate yourself so you can be the best you can be and better. Put the small things behind you and reach for your goal.

BEST WAY TO STAY FOCUSED: I focus on my horse, the task at hand and what my trainer and family are telling me. I try not to pay attention to the competition. I keep a picture perfect image of me and my horse in my head. I run through my pattern in my head over and over again, visualizing each perfect transition. I concentrate on myself and what I am doing at all times. Another thing is don't get nervous. Do the best you can and have fun!

MOST MEANINGFUL SHOW RING EXPERIENCE: 1998 Region V Show. I had just been riding Forgery about 4-5 weeks. I felt extremely confident and right on key. Forgery was right on the money the entire time. He felt so good and I just had to smile! When the Top Five lined up, the announcer said the judges wanted to compliment this very large and high quality class. Then she called Forgery and me forward as the Unanimous Champions in the Half-Arabian Country English Pleasure JTR.

Exerpted from Arabian Horse Times, July 1999, pages 63-64

What were the results of all of this time, work, money, and energy?

At the 1999 Arabian and Half-Arabian Youth National Championship show, Leslie won the following:

- National Champion Half-Arabian Country English Pleasureó Junior Owner to Ride (14-17)
- National Champion Half-Arabian Country English Pleasureó Junior to Ride (14-17)
- U.S. Top Ten Arabian Country English Pleasureó Junior to Ride (14-17)

She rode two different horses and worked hard and it paid off!

Prayer can obtain everything: it can open the windows of heaven, and shut the gates of hell; it can put a holy constraint upon God, and detain an angel until he leave a blessing.

~Mrs. Charles Cowman

God wants us to ask Him for the impossible! God can do things that man cannot do. He would not be God if this were not so. That is why He has graciously made prayer a law of life. "If you will ask...I will do." This inviting promise from the Lord means that He will do for us what we cannot do for ourselves; He will do for others what we cannot do for them - if we but ask Him.

~Mrs. Charles Cowman

Lord, teach us to pray. Some of us are not skilled in the art of prayer. As we draw near to thee in thought, our spirits long for thy Spirit, and reach out for thee, longing to feel thee near.

~Peter Marshall

...Now by this I know that thou art a man of God, and that the word of the Lord in thy mouth is truth.

~1 Kings 17:24

I know also, my God, that thou triest the heart, and hast plea-sure in uprightness. As for me, in the uprightness of mine heart I have willingly offered all these things: and now have I seen with joy thy people which are present here, to offer willingly unto thee.

~1 Chronicles 29:17

In Christ we are not promised "freedom from," instead we are promised that through divinely designed restrictions we are free to find what we yearn for: fulfillment and meaning in life. Slaves to Christ, we become truly free.

~Larry Richards

Success American Style

Seeing then that all these things shall be dissolved, what manner of persons ought ye to be in all holy conversation and godliness.

II Peter 3:11

11
Hope, You And The American Dream

I was recently sent this quote by one of my students:

"A man who has health has hope,
A man who has hope has everything!"

~Ancient Proverb

Hope excites passion. It is indispensable to success. In this chapter you find enthusiasm embedded in these sayings. You read an inspiring letter and an interview between Bill Mize and myself. Hope is essential to the success of all great undertakings.

Success American Style

Dear Wade:

I wish to thank you for your wonderful contributions. I'm writing not only to express my gratefulness, but to share an experience I had about two weeks ago that has more to do with the human experience than directly with financial success. On a Friday your tape arrived and I was wondering when I was going to find the time to listen to it. At 1:00 a.m. that very next morning there was an emergency call for me (I am a practicing vascular surgeon of 20 years). And I was groggily dreading another sleep-deprived weekend. On the way to the hospital, I heard most of the new tape, and was amazed at the transformation of how I felt. By now I was fully awake, alert, refreshed, and eagerly anticipating what lay in store.

I now realize what took place. You gave me something very important that early morning. That something is HOPE. Hope, one of our most powerful emotions, is the essence of motivation, and is priceless. Hope means different things to different people, but to me it means the promise of a less demanding professional life, of a life actually being with my family, of being able to retire from medicine rather than being retired by it, of financial security in essence. Hope is the future!

I profoundly thank you for rekindling that spirit that is within us all. Moreover, you are providing the power through which hope is operative. That power is EDUCATION, that engine we need to move us forward. Education is inestimable and irredeemable. You have that unique ability to make complex matters seem readily comprehensible. As a surgical educator I know what a rare gift this is. Again, I thank you for sharing your special talents.

Sincerely,
J.K., M.D.
Oregon

Hope, You And The American Dream

Whatever your hand finds to do, do it with your might.

~Ecclesiastes 9:10

You see things; and you say "Why?" But I dream things that never were; and I say, "Why not?"

~George Bernard Shaw

Work hard, be persistent and follow your dreams!

~Kerri Strug, Olympic Gold Medalist

America is the greatest country in the world. You can be anything you want to be within the laws of God and man. You can make your dreams come true if you work hard, stay focused on your goal and give back to the community that supports you.

~R. David Thomas

Every young person in America should believe that with God's help, he or she can make a great difference for good - both in America and throughout the world.

~Reverend Theodore M. Hesburgh

If your actions create a legacy that inspires others to dream more, learn more, do more and become more, then, you are an excellent leader.

~Dolly Parton

Personal excellence can be achieved by a visionary goal, thorough planning, dedicated execution and total follow through.

~Gerald R. Ford

But this I say, He which soweth sparingly shall reap also sparingly; and he which soweth bountifully shall reap also bountifully.

~2 Corinthians 9:6

105

Success American Style

I have been young, and now am old; yet have I not seen the righteous forsaken, nor his seed begging bread. He is ever merciful, and lendeth; and his seed is blessed.

~Psalm 37:25-26

Optimism is a [medicine.] Pessimism is a poison. Admittedly, every businessman must be realistic. He must gather facts, analyze them candidly and strive to draw logical conclusions, whether favorable or unfavorable. He must not engage in self-delusion. He must not view everything through rose-colored glasses. Granting this, the incontestable truth is that America has been built up by optimists. Not by pessimists, but by men possessing courage, confidence in the nation's destiny, by men willing to adventure, to shoulder risks terrifying to the timid.

~B. C. Forbes

The trouble with most people is that they're thinking with their hopes or fears or wishes rather than with their minds.

~Will Durant

People often say that this or that person has not yet found himself. But the self is not something that one finds. IT is something that one creates.

~Thomas Szasz

There is always hope in a man who actually and earnestly works. In idleness alone is there perpetual despair.

~Thomas Carlyle

To accept good advice is but to increase one's own ability.

~Johann Wolfgang Von Goethe

Hope, You And The American Dream

The following is an excerpt from a live interview with Wade Cook and Bill Mize on 9/27/99.

Wade: We have a unique experience here today. I was able to meet a gentleman, that was one of our students, okay his name is Bill Mize and I would like all of you to meet him and I'm going to have him sit here. I'm going to do an interview with him that I think our customers need to hear Bill's story. Okay, would you please listen very carefully as we go through this. Bill Mize it's good to have you here.

Bill: I appreciate it. My wife and I had always considered ourselves extremely conservative, we knew we were never going to be wealthy people, and we had no aspirations necessarily to being wealthy people. I was in law enforcement, my wife was a teacher and that's just two professions you don't go into if you're looking to make a lot of money. After about 17 years of marriage we had managed to amass a little over $80,000 and quite frankly we're pretty shocked even that we were able to do that. But primarily it was for our boy's future. I mean that was what our goal was early on. We had sort of set a goal to where we would limit what we did. Primarily our focus was toward our two boys and then about four years ago I was diagnosed with cancer and the doctors say that it is terminal. First diagnosis now, I mean I wish I could say it for a certainty its not even wishful thinking at a gut instinctual level I just don't believe them. After about four months and some additional testing they found out it was much more advanced than what it was initially.

Wade: And this is Hodgkin's disease. So the point is though that you took your $80,000 and started paying some of your own medical things.

Bill: We grew up in a real small town and we had always told my boys that if you had a bill and had the money, to pay it when the bill came in. Well, once insurance quit paying for the treatments that I was taking, it took four months for me to go from $82,000 down to about $8,500. I don't know if it was the magical figure of $8,500 or it was all of a sudden I had 10% left at that point I realized that the only way I could justify that was if I cared more about the doctors and the hospitals and all that, than I did my own children, because I could see that I was taking their entire inheritance and handing it over to people that I didn't know.

Wade: So you're down to $8,000. How old are your two boys?

Bill: My oldest boy is 16 and my youngest 13. At the time, that was three years ago, they were 10 and 13.

Wade: But over this last little while you have gotten your boys into the stock market, correct? Why do you want them to learn how to trade in the stock market?

Bill: Basically it was a case of the old adage of getting them fish or teaching them to fish. Your refer to it in your books and it's a case of what the doctors at that point were telling me. In fact I'm about a year past my death date according to the doctors.

Wade: Coming out to these seminars just keep you alive a lot longer because you always have to be someplace.

Bill: You'd be surprised how creative you can get trying to get to some of these classes. Well, I had my wife sneak me out of the hospital to come to this one.

Wade: Now you're a Cook University student but I don't want to go there yet. I want to go ahead and finish the answer why do you want your boys to trade.

Bill: I took $8,000, got with an attorney who's a friend of mine and he agreed to set up a trust in the boys' names. Like I said, I come from Arkansas and it is a community property state so anything that is in my name is in my wife's name. As my bills mount up it goes to her and it can't go to the next generation. So I took $5,000 of the $8,000 plus and put it, $2,500, into each boy's name in a trust account and the rest I used to pay for my Wall Street Workshop™. The boys are doing really well. They are still using the same elementary strategies they started with. They are doing rolling stocks and covered calls.

Wade: It has been about four months now, where are they?

Bill: We started the end of June and are actually using money now, we did five months of paper trading where they had to do a deal everyday.

Wade: I want everybody to hear this. What he had his two sons do when they were doing paper trading was to call him on his cell phone wherever they were, even if they were at school. He pretended he was their stockbroker and had the boys place trades with him.

Bill: Early on my wife was dead set against this because she knew what I was doing. She knew that I was preparing them for when I'm not around and she looked at that like I was giving up and you know her concern was that as soon as I got them where they could do it without me then it would be like okay I've accomplished what I want and I'm done.

Wade: So how has your 16-year-old done? What is the $2,500 worth now?

Bill: He actually has not done as well as the 13-year-old. He is up to about $3,900.

Wade: And the 13-year-old?

Bill: He is up to about $4,300.

Wade: In about four months?

Bill: Right, but it's very active for them. We're doing it where we are writing the covered call, buying it back and actively playing them. We are not just sitting and watching them.

Wade: So you obviously believe in education I mean education in your law enforcement career, education here and now do your sons believe in it as much as you do?

Bill: Yes, absolutely.

Wade: Your relationship with your family is now so much better?

Bill: Oh it's unbelievable. In fact, I was telling some people that during the Trade Forge class, every week I go have lunch with my boys at school. My 16 year old, he's liking that less and less and we we're going to have to work it out where I pick him up and we go but you know when they were younger, like I said when all this started whey they were 13 and 10 it was like, man this is cool you're the only Dad that comes up here and has lunch with us and you could tell that it was that it meant something and I thought, look what I missed out on all because I was more concerned with other things.

Wade: They weren't hugging your wallet they were hugging you.

Bill: Right, they would have rather had me than any amount of money and I didn't see it.

Wade: So your $80,000 was down to $8,000 and now they have $2,500 back up to around $4,000 each and you're hoping that they will just continue with this and pay their own way through college and do well. Last question, what do you see now for you and your family?

Bill: The freedom that it gives them. If it's not college they want to do or start a business, they've got something that is a ready income. They know the key is knowledge. I am absolutely enjoying every second of everyday of the next twenty years of my life and I think that's what I'll take out of this.

Wade: Thanks Bill. We appreciate you being here.

12
Pledge Of Allegiance

If one asks me the meaning of our flag, I say to him: It means all that the Constitution of our people, organizing for justice, for liberty and for happiness, meant.

Our Flag carries American ideas, American history, and American feelings.

This American Flag was the safeguard of liberty. It was an ordinance of liberty by the people, for the people. That it meant, that it means, and, by the blessing of God, that it shall mean to the end of time!

~Henry Ward Beecher

The Original Pledge of Allegiance

> I pledge allegiance to my Flag,
> And the Republic for which it stands,
> One nation indivisible - with liberty
> And justice for all.

> > ~Francis Bellamy, 1892

At the first National Flag Conference in Washington D.C., on June 14, 1923, a change was made for clarity: the words "the Flag of the United States" replaced "my flag."

In 1942 Congress officially recognized the Pledge of Allegiance.

In June of 1954 an amendment was made to add the words "under God." President Dwight D. Eisenhower said, "In this way we are reaffirming the transcendence of religious faith in America's heritage and future; in this way we shall constantly strengthen those spiritual weapons which forever will be our country's most powerful resource in peace and war."

The Pledge of Allegiance

> I pledge allegiance to the flag
> of the United States of America and
> to the Republic for which it stands,
> one nation under God,
> indivisible, with liberty and
> justice for all.

The following is an excerpt from *Light of Liberty* by Paul H. Dunn. Used with permission.

I Pledge Allegiance

As Americans, both you and I have stood with thousands of others and repeated the Pledge of Allegiance. As I have pondered the material for this book, I have considered seriously the implications of what allegiance is all about. We use the term so easily, so lightly, and yet I have a feeling that perhaps this is wrong.

I have wondered if perhaps the time may come when we will all be required to "pledge our allegiance" with more than our words.

A review of the beginnings of this great nation confirms the fact that allegiance can be costly. The fifty-six signers of the Declaration of Independence are a perfect example of what it means to pledge allegiance to this flag of ours:

Five signers were captured by the British as traitors, and tortured before they died. Twelve had their homes ransacked and burned. Two lost their sons in the Revolutionary Army; another had two sons captured. Nine of the fifty-six fought and died from wounds or the hardship of the Revolutionary War.

What kind of men were they? Twenty-four were lawyers and jurists. Eleven were merchants, nine were farmers and large plantation owners, men of means and well educated. But they signed the Declaration of Independence knowing full well that the penalty would be death if they were captured.

These were not wild-eyed, rabble-rousing ruffians; they were soft-spoken men of means and education. They had security, but they valued liberty more.

Although there was no official "Pledge of Allegiance" for these great patriots, they put into words their own pledge. Their statement of allegiance has been memorized and quoted ever since. Here are those memorable words:

Success American Style

"For the support of this declaration, with a firm reliance on the protection of Divine Providence, we mutually pledge to each other, our lives, our fortunes, and our sacred honor."

And they meant it! Somehow I can't believe that those fifty-six Americans all expected to pay the price they did. But the fact that they were willing to do so is remarkable.

Since the time of our founding fathers, men and women have continued to pledge their lives, their fortunes, and their sacred honor.

Abraham Lincoln pledged his all for our country and he gave it. But even before his assassination, he knew what it meant to give-and not to be appreciated. Giving our lives, our fortunes, and our honor is not always noted. Nevertheless, since Lincoln's time, hundreds of thousands of valiant Americans have continued to do so. Thousands upon thousands did so in World War I. They continued to do so in World War II, in Korea, in Vietnam, in Lebanon, in Desert Storm, throughout all the world. While there are some-such as President John F. Kennedy and his brother Robert, together with Martin Luther King and others-who have been recognized for their ultimate sacrifice, there have been many unnumbered Americans who have quietly gone about making their sacrifices in innumerable ways, many even giving their lives, without acknowledgment.

What makes men willing to pledge their lives to this country? I believe President Lincoln knew. So did the thousands of others who have joined him in death for the cause of truth and freedom. Lincoln said:

"This love of liberty which God has planted in us constitutes the bulwark of our liberty and independence. It is not our form in battlements, or bristling sea coasts, or only in our Navy. Our defense is in the spirit which prizes liberty as the heritage of all men in all lands everywhere. Destroy this spirit, and we have planted the seeds of despotism at our own doors."

It is the love of liberty which motivates our allegiance to America. God planted it in all of us. If we nurture it, it never dies. What do we do to make sure the light and spirit of liberty within each of us does remain? What will make us "pledge our allegiance" unwaveringly to this nation? Laying down our lives may not be necessary. In fact, I pray that we may never be required to do so. But in one way or another we can do something-many things-to keep that spirit alive.

We can carefully examine our lives and see what needs to be spent to keep the spirit of liberty alive in our hearts. Here are some simple choices. We can:

1. Vote.

2. Attend our neighborhood mass meetings.

3. Keep track of our political representatives and write to them when appropriate.

4. Display the flag on special occasions (or even daily).

5. Pray for our elected officials, especially the president of our country.

6. Teach our children to love this great nation.

7. Pay an honest income tax (now there's a challenge for some)!

8. Obey the laws of the land.

9. Run for office.

10. Talk positively about the freedoms we enjoy.

The list goes on. You and I can do at least some of these things.

God has truly implanted in each one of us the spirit of liberty. If we're true to that spirit, we'll be all right. In fact, we'll be great! Our allegiance may be demonstrated in small ways, or we may be called upon to give our lives. But either way, I bear witness that God will know of our sacrifice, and He will reward us personally and as a country, both now and forever.

May I, with you, take this opportunity once again to pledge my great love, support, and loyalty for and to the United States of America; and may we, together, hold fast and firm to this promise, for our own sakes and for the sake of this nation.

Appendix
The All-American Pastime

Hi, my name is Carl Sanders. I have known Wade for about 2½ years, and am currently working as an Executive for the Stock Market Institute of Learning. I was so pleased when Wade talked about writing this book. I have been repeatedly moved by Wade's patriotism, and hope that you too will be a far more sensitive and committed American after reading this book. He dearly loves this country and is always sharing quotes from this country's founding fathers. Thank you, Wade for your fervent example.

I know that the focus of this book is about the greatness of America, and I know no better "only-in-America" success story than Wade Cook. Wade's story truly is a rags to riches story at its finest. The best thing about Wade's success, however, is that he is freely sharing with "average Joe and Joan Americans" exactly the strategies that he used and still uses today that have made him a multimillionaire. Because of this, many of our students have also proven out these strategies which has enabled them to live the American Dream for themselves. One of the things that makes America so great is the opportunities she provides for all of us. With the opportunity to succeed all you then need is the know-how and (even a small bit of) capital to get started.

Because Wade's strategies work, and make so much sense, I wanted everyone reading this book to be presented with the opportunity to enhance their life with more cash flow. Recently Wade wrote a great special report wherein he, in very easy to understand terms, drew some powerful correlations between the stock market and baseball. This report introduces some of Wade's basic stock market strategy concepts and has been so well received.

Even though Wade wanted this book to focus people's attention of the greatness of America, we had a discussion about the many students of ours who are living the American dream, and I encouraged Wade to also include his recent special report. Begin to learn these strategies: read this special report. It's what the American dream is all about. I hope you enjoy this special report letter.

Baseball, the Stock Market and You

Whoever wants to know the heart and mind of America had better learn baseball.

~Jacques Barzun

Baseball is a great sport. It has thrilled fans for decades. It has been good to its players, leaving many rich, some famous, but nearly all enriched and fulfilled. It has been a wonderful slice of the American pie.

There are so many things to learn from baseball that apply to life. Lessons from baseball can even help us with stock market investing. I know this seems like a stretch, but follow me through this report and hopefully you'll make more money in the market.

Now, I've just made a leap in my own judgement about you; that maybe your opinion of the stock market, or about investments in general, might cause you to miss out on opportunities. What I would like to do is make a case for a different way of looking at, and a different way of using the stock market. I don't think you have ever read or heard anything like this, so I sincerely encourage you to hear me out.

Before I get on to this new angle to the stock market, let me first express my style, basically who I am. I want to be one of the country's best educators. I love the financial arena. It's not only my career, but my hobby and I have a passion for it. Luckily, I've found ways to "cash flow" the market. I've written books and now whole courses on my style of formulas or methods for creating income.

My passion was not to get rich, but to be a great teacher. If you are to judge me in this endeavor, it must start here in this report, not after you've read a book or attended one of my workshops. So, as you read you will learn a few basic formulas. I hope by doing so you will find yourself thinking, "<u>I can do this</u>, I don't have to work from 8 to 5 for the next 30 years. I can spend more time with my family or I can give more to my church." You see, the measurement of my job is simple. It is not to see how much I can put into you, but to see how much I can <u>get out of you</u>. The good part for you is that even though you might be a beginner, you can learn ways to build income. Yes, even enough income so you can <u>quit your job</u>. What you learn is financial freedom.

You could read that last part as: Wade's job is to educate me. I learn these cash flow methods which I don't currently know or understand, I apply them and then I get to keep all my profits, quit my job and live a freer life. We're talking about results, <u>tangible</u>, <u>spendable results</u>. This is not about getting rich, but about making an extra $3,000 to $12,000 per month.

To start the process, reason with me on this next question: <u>Is the stock market the solution to your income problems</u>? Good question. For most people, the stock market (the way most people look at it and invest in it) is not a viable solution to paying the bills and buying a new home. Seriously, who do you know who has quit their job (including your stockbroker) from cash flow generated from the market? Did you even come up with one? I know many. They are my students and we have drawers full of testimonials to prove it. Look at just one from Joel. <u>He literally paid off his house</u>.

Appendix: The All-American Pastime

"A year ago we didn't know if we were going to keep this house. Today it's paid for. All due to the lessons we learned at [Stock Market Institute of Learning]! We made $230,079, today January 12, 1999. We made it on CMGI. A tech stock. In fact, on January 11th, we made $47,855, and on January 7th, we made $46,644. We've made $372,725, in just the opening days of this month. We've never lost a dime when we followed the rules as taught at the Wall Street Workshop™. We had no background, Zero, Zip, Nada experience playing stocks before Wade. I don't think it's that he's done something new. What he's done is put it into plain language us common folk can understand."

-Joel & Jennifer Diamond, CA

Okay, so who am I and what does this mean to you? My name is Wade Cook. I was born and raised in Tacoma, Washington. In my early twenties, I was an insurance agent. At first I drove a cab to make ends meet and I learned quickly that big, continuous profits could be made by taking numerous smaller runs rather than waiting for the big ones. The "meter drop" method was born.

I started buying junky old houses but instead of using them as rentals or trying to get maximum dollars in selling them, I quickly fixed them up, sold below full retail value and usually carried the mortgage (owner financing). Soon I had many contracts with monthly checks coming in that generated enough income for me to retire at the age of 29.

Years later when the real estate market took a hit (mid 80s) I started applying the "meter drop" to the stock market. I changed baseball fields three times but the rules are still essentially the same. I still love real estate but my heart is in the stock market. Real estate was a means to an end; so is the stock market.

Baseball is the only field of endeavor where a man can succeed three times out of ten and be considered a good performer.

~Ted Williams

The stock market is easy to trade in. Now, I didn't say it's easy to make a profit in, because just as in any business you need to learn the ropes, study, practice and <u>surround yourself with a good team</u>. So, by easy I mean you can do it on a cell phone, on a computer in your car or in the back bedroom. Investing in the market has risks, but not the traditional expenses of owning your own business. There is no rent, no insurance, no employees, no advertising or any of the other thousands of expenses, distractions and competition most businesses face.

Treat it Like a Business

So now that I've bad-mouthed having your own business, let me bring up a conundrum. Most fortunes are created by venturing out, by having your own business or enterprise. Very few fortunes are created by employees working for big or small companies. Wealth is in ownership. That's why I have repeatedly said that the stock market makes a great full or part-time business as long as we treat it like a business. You'll note that I didn't say treat it like a job. We'll talk about treating it like a job later.

Baseball is a game, yes. It is also a business.

~Willie Mays

As an active stockbroker, I did not take my first Wall Street Workshop™ based solely on my thirst for knowledge. It was only after persistent urging, and nagging, from my brother, a graduate of the Wall Street Workshop™, did I decide to finally attend. He consistently made money in the stock market after he attended the Wall Street Workshop. Quit his job, making more money in the market using the short-term "meter drop" than I did using the long-term buy and hold. So I decided I might have some time to learn how the "meter drop" works.

I am now eternally grateful to my brother for all the harassing phone calls he placed to me trying to convince me to attend the Wall Street Workshop. And that I didn't have all the answers - that took some convincing. After I reached the point I was making more money in the market than I did as a broker with over 800 clients, I quit my job. I now have the satisfaction and peace of mind of knowing that with the right knowledge and education I received by coming to all the classes offered by Wade that I will never have to work a day in my life again."

~Stacy Acevedo

Run #1: We are educators. Period. Tell your stockbroker that we are not trying to steal you as a client. In fact, we want you to learn these formulas and types of trades so you and your broker can work better together. Notice that I use a real live stockbroker and will encourage you to do so also. Online trading is too darn expensive. A good stockbroker makes you money, more than they cost.

Let the critics roar, we keep on helping people make more and keep more of what they make. The critics keep us thinking and improving. This benefits our students in numerous ways. We help a lot of people consistently hit singles. <u>Now you're on first base</u>.

Run #2: We're into formulas (techniques, methods, et cetera) which produce <u>repetitive</u> cash flow. Might I add repetitive, safe and <u>real spendable cash</u>.

We don't sell investments. We don't get anything out of what our students make. I know this is tough for a few government authorities to take because they want to lump us together with traditional investment firms. More on how we're different later. It's time for you to learn "what's available" (see Run #4). On page 126-127, I'll put in the left column the age old formula that virtually all mutual funds, brokers, financial planners use. In the right column I'll list the 13 formulas taught at our Wall Street Workshop™. Note: Seven of the thirteen are major strategies wherein we use the "tell, show, do" teaching format. The other six minor strategies are taught but with less emphasis. <u>You now have a runner on first and second</u>.

Run #3: Let me get in another friendly jab at my critics and virtually all the financial journalists in newspapers and magazines. I wonder, when I read their comments about me, why they never take me on and debate the mechanics of a formula, or criticize my methods. The closest they come to doing this is to discount options trading as risky. For the most part, however, they dwell on something in my life that happened 15 years ago. I guess they figure if they can't kill the message, attack the messenger.

I also wonder if they think that everyone in America has <u>five to ten million dollars</u> to invest. If you read their articles and try to figure out their methods, I think you'll also gain this opinion. Seriously, they give nothing, show nothing, teach nothing for the little guy.

Appendix: The All-American Pastime

You see, the people who are attracted to me can sometimes only scrape together $5,000 to $25,000 to invest, sometimes more, but more often even less. Most of these journalists/financial gurus won't even take on accounts less than $50,000 to $100,000. You can tell their elitist attitude when they start talking about "asset allocation." Now don't get me wrong, this level of thinking is good and right for some people. They say things like this: Put 30% of your money in growth stocks; 20% into large value stocks; 20% into foreign stocks; 10% into bonds and 20% into cash. My goodness. My students, starting with $2,000 or $7,000 can't even relate; $2,000 divided up this way is inappropriate.

I say learn one formula at first to get started. If you're a beginner this formula should require little cash, i.e., Rolling Stocks, Writing Covered Calls. Study it extensively, Practice thoroughly with paper trades, Understand it well, then Do. That's the SPUD way. I was going to say this SPUD's for you, but I don't want to be too cliché.

Asset Allocation-Humbug. How about formula allocation? If you have $10,000, put $2,000 into rolling stocks, $7,000 into great stocks for writing covered calls and $1,000 into an option play on a company doing a stock split. If you're going to play options, do ten $1,000 trades or five $2,000 trades.

Many of my students have millions of dollars, but most start with very little. Read the testimonial on the next page by Jodi Larkin. She started with $200. I applaud her determination. If she had read the wrong headed advice by my detractors where would she be?

In short, there are three reasons for investing: cash flow, tax write-offs and growth. I say cash flow is paramount. You can buy all the tax

The Rest of the Guys	*The Wade Cook Way*

1. Long-term hold
  a. Blue Chip Stocks
  b. Bargain Stocks
  c. Mutual Funds, REITS, et cetera
	1. Long-term hold
	  a. Blue Chip Stocks
	  b. Bargain Stocks
	  c. Mutual Funds, REITS, et cetera

	2. Rolling Stocks Buy and selll on repeated and predictable patterns (highs and lows).
	3. Options Proxy investing-low cost, limited risk options for safety investing.
	4. Writing Covered Calls Generate income monthly on stocks you own or buy.
	5. Stock Splits (and other news) There are five strategies to enter and exit stocks or options doing splits.
	6. Sell Puts Generate income-get paid now.
	7. Bull Put Spreads Generate income, limit risk, lessen margin.

The Rest of the Guys	*The Wade Cook Way*
	8. Bull Call Spreads Writing covered calls by covering with options.
	9. Bargain Hunting Bottom fishing for long-term hold or quick pops.
	10. Spin-offs Capture the stock-buy options on stock.
	11. IPOs If not at first, wait, get in and out. Use 25 day IPO rule.
	12. Turnarounds Catch the wave up and do stocks or proxy investing.
	13. Slams and Peaks (Really two strate-gies.) Catch the turn one to five day plays. Quick cash.
This comparison explains itself. We realize it's embarrassing for those other guys and we humbly invite them to come to our Wall Street Workshop™ and learn how to use these methods for themselves.	14. Range Riders (Bonus Strategy) Buy and sell at tops and bottoms all the way up.

write-offs you want later. Learn how to generate income now and you can buy all the growth you want later. Concentrate on cash flow. Your need for income will only increase as your need for tax shelters and growth change.

What I'm into is building steady and safe monthly income. You've heard of PMA (Positive Mental Attitude), well I'm into PMI (Perpetual Monthly Income). I submit that it's easy to have a PMA when you have PMI.

One more testimonial from a stockbroker who knew those formulas (ways of actually making money) existed, but didn't learn them in the typical stockbroker training program.

"Prior to attending the Wall Street Workshop, I was familiar with the stock market, and had done covered calls as far back as the mid 1970s. I have held seven securities licenses since 1969, and in 1987, I worked on the trading desk at a discount stock brokerage firm.

With all that as a background, I must admit that my experience with the workshop not only expanded my knowledge base, but more importantly enhanced my motivation to improve my trading comfort level.

In my years of contact with the field of finance, I have observed that ignorance is expensive on many occasions."

~Bob Zimmerman, MI

Stock Splits

If you have heard of me at all, you no doubt have heard me talk or read my writings about stock splits. We have become very sophisticated in our profit making approaches to these events.

Appendix: The All-American Pastime

Overall most stocks going through stock splits do very well. I've put forth a challenge to find a company's stock which has not regained or rebounded to the original price within two, three or four years. There are a few-very few. If anyone can find one I'll show you 50 to 100 which have gone back up within one year. Read this again. If I'm right, then investing in these companies (either by buying the stock or by using low-cost, limited-risk options) could be quite profitable.

The long-term potential is quite awesome, especially if earnings are increasing and the company has a history or pattern of doing splits. But what about short-term, quick turn plays. I have isolated five specific times to play stock splits. These are designed to be one day to one month trades-quick in and quick out. Never go in the entrance until you know the exit.

Back to a baseball comparison. The hitting line-up is very important to success. The first four or five batters are crucial to getting scores. It's called the power part of the line-up. The fourth batter is called the clean-up hitter. The first three batters are to get on base-even if it's a walk. If they can get one or two of the batters on, then number four comes in and hopefully cleans-up. This comparison can only go so far as each option play has a beginning and an ending. One play does not need a clean-up hitter to drive it around the diamond. However, my favorite is stock split strategy number four.

First of all look at these four charts on stock splits. Look at the prices of the stocks going back up to the pre-split price. Second, these trades can be profitable by playing the stocks but hugely profitable with cheaper options. Let's explore options. See *Wall Street Money Machine*, *Stock Market Miracles*, *Safety 1st Investing* by Wade Cook, and Bob Eldridge's *Mak-*

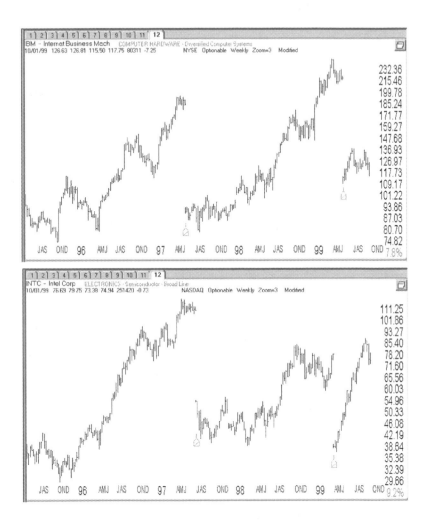

ing a Living in the Stock Market - all available
at your favorite bookstore.

Stock options are one way of locking down the
price of a stock for a set period of time. It's
September, you like Microsoft. You buy an option
to buy Microsoft at $95 on or before the 3rd

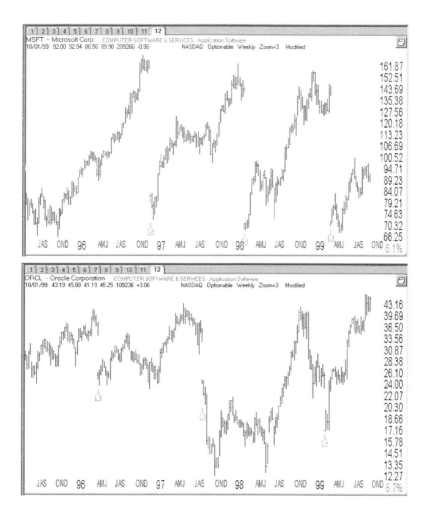

Friday of November, for $100 on or before the 3rd Friday of January, 2000.

The November call options (the right to buy) give you the right, but not the obligation, to buy the stock for $95. That's the strike price. You could have chosen $90, $85 or even $100. We spend a lot of time at the Wall Street Workshop™ showing you the different choices and helping you Simutrade™ (on paper, with monopoly-like money) to prepare yourself for success. The stock is at $94.

The $95 calls are going for $6. If you buy one contract that would be $600 plus commissions. If you want to control 1,000 shares, that would require 10 contracts (100 shares each) and $6,000. Just think, for just $6,000 you control 1,000 shares of Microsoft at the $95 price. Now, I don't buy options to buy the stock, I buy options so as they increase in value, I can sell for a profit. This is hard for some people to understand. If Microsoft goes up, say $3, my option could go up $1 to $2. I could sell the option (it takes less than 30 seconds to sell) for $8 or $8,000. My $6,000 has turned to $8,000 in a few days or weeks. Sometimes it happens within hours. You would have made $4,000 on the stock, but you would have had to put up $94,000 in cash or $47,000 on margin. Not a bad return. But with low- cost, limited-risk options you only put up $6,000 not $94,000. A $2,000 profit on $6,000 is far superior to a $4,000 profit on $47,000 or $94,000.

What about the downside, you ask? Here's the good part. If everything tanked, you can only lose your invested amount, say the $3,000 or $6,000. If Microsoft goes to $85 and never re- covers you could lose the whole option amount, but you'll learn to put in stop orders at 50%. Anyway, what about the stock? Your $94 stock is down to $85 a $9,000 loss. Most stockbrokers think nothing of putting you into risky stocks (especially some of those non-earning Internet stocks) and bad mouth options as risky. Don't be fooled. If Microsoft takes off to say $108 your $95 call option could be worth $18, or $18,000. $6,000 to $18,000 - WOW. Tell me where you can get limited downside risk and unlimited upside potential? Options definitely have their place.

Let's explore an option and a stock split. When the stock splits, the option splits. Your $6,000 purchases 10 contracts at a strike price of $95. After the split you have 20 contracts with a strike price of $47.50. Do you like this? Your cost basis is $3 per option. If you purchase 10 $90 call options and the company announces a 3:1 stock split you will end up with 30 contracts with a strike price of $30. Pretty cool indeed.

Now, let's play ball. Stock split strategies as batters.

Batter #1 - Pre-announcement. These stocks run in groups, one splits, many follow. Many companies split when their stock gets to a certain price. Many split about the same time, or pattern - say every 15 months. This is an awesome strategy if you get in early.

Batter #2 - On the announcement. This time is very dangerous. The option premiums (the implied volatility or speculative value) get so pricey. Be careful. Maybe you should be a seller, not a buyer.

Batter #3 - Between the announcement and the split (usually four to six weeks after the announcement). Many of these stocks back off after the initial run up and then form roll patterns. This gives many buy and sell opportunities.

Batter #4 - The Clean up Hitter

(A) Rally into the split. If the split date is Friday (also called the pay date), then the ex-dividend date is Monday; the $100 shares on Friday open on Monday at around $50. On Wednesday, or so, before the split Friday, after the stock has backed off from say a high of $105, and is now $94, we hope for a rally. If the stock goes up to $98 or even $102 by Friday, we're out. This is a quick one to three day trade. A $4,000 $95 call turns into $6,000 by Friday mid-morning. Sell, the play is over—a $2,000 profit.

(B) I've noticed that most stocks back off after the split-or on the split date or in a few days. The stock goes to $102 and opens Monday at $51. Buy a put, or clean out stock and call option positions. Buy back in later when the stock bottoms at $46 and heads on to the next news reporting time of the quarterly cycle.

4A and 4B are two sides of the same coin. They are predictable. They are visible signs which you can get good at observing. There are clean entrance and exit points.

Batters 5 through 9 are all the different plays, short-term and long-term (LEAPS®) after the stock has done the split.

These batters win games. They allow our students to quit their jobs, generate income, give more to their churches and charities. The emphasis is on selling-cleaning out before the value deteriorates and falls. These strategies put the emphasis on selling, not on buying. We only buy so we have something to sell. These methods are <u>learnable</u> and <u>repeatable</u>. They will help you increase the quality of your life.

Now, what does this mean to you? Well you should know that formulas exist and these formulas are to be used in different situations. Each one is learnable and usable. Each one either carries with it a certain risk or is designed to minimize risk (my favorite).

Run #4: <u>I'm into learning</u>. There is an old proverb that says, "When the student is ready the teacher appears." I'm into helping my students/customers learn. We use a remarkably effective method of teaching/learning. It's called experiential learning. We get the student as close to the real life experience as possible. We use a three stage format and have now helped over 64,000 people (attendees at our Wall Street Workshops™) get up and get going in the market. (Note: Our format is three fold. We Tell, Show and Do.)

The Wall Street Workshop™ effectiveness is that in many classes around 32% are referrals from previous students. They can't wait to get home and start trading. When their family members and friends see their cash flow results, they want to come too.

"In October 1998 I signed up for the workshop. I started trading the second day and on the third day (Friday) had made a 52.44% return. Not too bad for one day of trading. I have continued to trade on my own plus with my friend who has a large amount of money in the market.

Most of my trades have been buying options. The trades I have done with my friend have been covered calls. Prior to trading with me, my friend just held on to the stock. The best trades I have shown him are on the stock CUBE. He bought 1,000 shares for $18/ share two years ago. Until this January he had no income from this stock. Since January he has sold the call for every month and twice in two months. His income was over $11,000 and he was called out in June for $25/share."

~Lee Stump, MN

Look at this-$11,000 of EXTRA cash flow!

Tell: Explain the strategy. Go through the definitions. Explain the rules and the process.

Success American Style

Show: Get current quotes (prices of stock and options) and do the deal-either real or paper. Then do another example, then another-in a Q & A discussion, format.

Do: Place a trade (real or Simutrade™)-again the Wall Street Workshop™ shows you how to practice perfectly. Practice doesn't make perfect-perfect practice makes perfect. Why would anyone put their money in harms way without working out the bugs-or paper trade. In fact, everyone should use the following guidelines of paper or simulated trading.

1. Paper trade each strategy at least 15 times and have 10 profitable trades (on paper) in a row before using real money.

2. Do five trades every day-paper or real. So if you don't have enough cash, then paper trade. When cash is freed up you will be in the flow and ready to go. Do practice basics every day.

3. When the market or a stock has a dramatic move, go back to paper until you figure out the new arena or trading ranges.

The Do or Deploy part of this process gives us a chance to watch over our student's progress. On the Seven Major Strategies, they're excused to go call their own brokers for prices and advice. Many brokers are not up on all aspects of these formulas. This Q & A time is often the most fun part of our two day Wall Street Workshop™.

The best baseball people are Cartesians. That is, they apply Descartes' methods to their craft, breaking it down into bite-size components. Mastering them and then building the craft up, bit by bit. . .Master enough little problems and you will have few big problems.

    ~George Will

Appendix: The All-American Pastime

The Tell, Show and Do format is a wonderful process that helps students get through the learning curve very quickly. Our job is not to make good Workshop attendees out of our students, but to make them good when they get home and are with their own trading professionals. You have a man on first, second and third. We need a home run.

I would like to now share with you a most curious thing that happened to me. I was scheduled to go into the recording studio. The topic was formula trading and how our Wall Street Workshop™ is the best training in the country. Actually, there's no one in second place. I thought long and hard on what I was to say. I put off the recording for several weeks. Finally, one morning, about 4 a.m. as I lay in bed it came to me. It was simple. I should get off my side of the fence, as an educator, and tell you what I would want, as a student, in a stock market workshop.

I lay there and came up with three things that I would want, even demand, from a seminar. Think these through with me and tell me what type of seminar/workshop you would design for yourself if you had the chance? Look at the chart on page 138 for a list of what we do compared to others.

First: I would want to know what's available. What type of trades can be made in different situations. Even though I might not know much about the market, I do realize there are beginning, intermediate and advanced methods. What can I use? Can I take the powerful formulas the "big guys" use (the major league players instead of the minor league players) and simplify them for my own benefit.

But to keep it simple, I thought, let's go back to basics. I'm just starting to learn baseball. There's one out, a runner on first and I've never played the infield. The coach yells, "Okay, double play-c'mon guys, double it up."

A Unique Comparison

YES, WE ARE DIFFERENT...

The following shows the major difference between Stock Market Institute of Learning and all the other financial professionals.

STOCKBROKERS FINANCIAL PLANNERS FUND MANAGERS	STOCK MARKET INSTITUTE OF LEARNING
1. They receive commissions for selling investments, regardless of returns to client.	1. We sell no investments. We teach strategies for wise decision making and the generation of cash flow. We get nothing out of what our students make.
2. They advise clients on specific investments.	2. We explain formulas, methods, and techniques to work the market. Stocks are mentioned as working examples. No specific advice is given.
3. Many financial professionals get paid a percentage of asset base they manage, whether assets increase or decrease.	3. We teach. The students learn and earn. They work the formulas, after paper or Simutrading™, and keep all the profits. We help investors choose better stockbrokers and how to work better with them.
4. They sometimes get investors involved in risky investments.	4. We show students how to avoid and minimize risk with a dedication to knowledge and specific tools like low-cost options, spreads, puts on increased values and writing covered calls.
5. They preach "asset allocation" placing portions of investor's money in harm's way.	5. We teach how to use a diversity of formulas for cash flow, tax write-offs, and growth. We help students learn to find certain stocks/options that fit the formulas.
6. They constantly sell investors the new "investment du jour."	6. We teach and show investors how to work the formulas, spread out risk, avoid losses and not get caught up in erratic and fad investments.

7. Some move money in and out to generate commissions.

7. We are an unbiased educational source. We get nothing out of what our students do. We only talk about a stock or option if it fits one of our cash flow or wealth building formulas.

8. Most do not show their trading results, they surely do not publicize their personal trades.

8. We tell all, show all. All trades are listed on our award winning Internet site at wadecook.com.* Current subscribers tap into this informative tutorial service.** Anyone can scroll back and see all trades (the when, where, how to, and why to).

9. Many are single-minded. They have their products for sale. They are concerned about their commissions with little regard for their client's complete financial picture or direction.

9. We teach, show and expound on five holistic financial topics:

A. We teach how to make money (actual cash flow) in business, in the stock market and in real estate.

B. We show how to reduce exposure to liability and risk through the use of different entities like:

• Nevada Corporations

• Pension Plans

• Living Trusts

• Family Limited Partnerships

• Charitable Remainder Trusts

C. We show how to reduce and pay less taxes.

D. We teach how to prepare for a great retirement.

E. We show how to effectively bequeath to loved ones (or charities) everything one has worked hard to build up.

*Chosen by readers of Securities Traders Handbook as the web site with the most new investment ideas.

**Website performance recognized by AT&T: Wade Cook Financial Corporation was recognized for its outstanding success by AT&T. The website, www.wadecook.com is hosted by AT&T.

Hey, sounds good, but what if I don't know what a forced out is? We just have to get a ground ball to second, touch second with our foot to force out the runner from first, and then throw the ball to first and the first baseman then only needs to touch the bag, or tag the runner before the runner gets to first base. Bam, double play. Two more outs-inning over. Again, can you do a double play if you do not know what a forced out is? That is what I mean by "know what is available."

I know this was a long example, but what if there are double plays in the stock market. Much like baseball with fixed plays and specific formulas on specific movements. What we do is teach the plays then our students work with their own advisors, for suitability and specific trade prices. The point is that you need to learn the rules. You won't know how to do a double play unless you know what a forced out is. Go back and look at our 13 Cash Flow Strategies. Do you know the rules, the specific techniques, better times to get in and out? In short, do you know the ropes?

Also in knowing what's available I want to know the jargon, or language so I don't do foolish things.

Second: I want to see the deals done. I want to see them done over and over again. I want examples. I want to see it work under different circumstances. I want to see when to get in and when to get out.

I want to see what happens when the trade doesn't go the way we planned. I want to study and practice the trades. I want to ask questions and move from knowledge or information to a true understanding.

<u>Third</u>: I want to do the deals myself. If paper trading or simulation trading will protect my money as I go through the learning curve, then fine, but I still want the experience to look and feel real. I realize that experience is the best teacher, but it's truly a wise person who can learn through the eyes (mistakes) of another.

Vernon Law, the famous baseball pitcher said, "Experience is expensive because it gives the test first, the lesson later." In short, I want to see, feel and get results. I want to move on to applications and learn how to keep practicing so when it's time to use real money, I'm ready with a wealth of knowledge and a chest full of understanding and I have done numerous trades to work out the kinks, build confidence and overcome fear.

I was excited to get into the studio that day. I was on our student's side of the fence. I practiced what I was to say all the way to the office. Then it dawned on me that I had just discovered the other side of the educational coin I was so dedicated to working. Look at the following.

<u>OUR EDUCATIONAL METHOD</u>	<u>WHAT I WANT AS A STUDENT</u>
1. TELL: Teach the strategies	1. Learn what's available-what works and when.
2. SHOW: Use examples, discuss, explore	2. Be shown examples and get explanations from someone who walks the walk.
3. DO: and watch over	3. Do the deals, with someone to help me understand how to get results.

Success American Style

Do you see why my enthusiasm was so high? As a matter of fact, it's high all the time because so many people benefit. Look at the following comments from our students.

"I took my first Wall Street Workshop™ in March of 1998. I quit my full-time job of 20 years in May of that same year. In the first two months of 1999 I made twice as much money as I earned at my former job in a year. I have helped two of my children buy homes, paid off the mortgage of my own home, paid cash for a car, a boat and a grand piano. I also have my food storage and a little gold. I am very confident at this point that I can make an excellent living in the stock market and never have a full-time job again."

-Steve Bunnell, WA

"I realize that I can retire today! I plan to do so and devote my full time to my young son and manage my portfolio. Today, I made my first trades based upon what I have learned from your course. While at your course, I decided to use only half my portfolio ($200,000) and to do only covered calls (for now). My total cash flow for today was $25,000 with a potential for another $19,250 for $5^1/_2$ weeks!"

~Susanna Ross Ryavec, OH

"I started trading about 4 months ago. I am an at home mom and wanted to generate monthly cash flow to help with the family bills. Using Wade Cook strategies on rolling stocks, I generated $1,000 per month. I came to the Wall Street Workshop™ to perfect my strategies so that I can reach my goal: Within 6 months I plan to earn enough monthly

income so that my husband can sell his business and join me at the computer to continue trading."

~Katie Johnson, FL

Now why do I bring this up here? You see, there are many (critics, some stockbrokers, journalists) who say, "Hey Americans, you're stupid. You can't understand the machinations of the market. Give your money to us. We'll manage it (for many fees). We have all the research, and methods. We'll take care of it for you."

Then along comes Wade Cook, a cab driver, who says, "Hold it Americans! You <u>are</u> smart enough. You <u>can</u> learn and do these things. You can take your financial life into your own hands." You can do it. I'll learn the formulas, distill them down and then help you learn them. You can do it without fancy computers. You can do it without a lot of money to get started. And you can do it in a way that keeps your money safe while you learn and then earn with your real money, "Safety 1st" is the byword. (Note: My book, *Safety 1st Investing* is at your bookstore now). When I show, explore, expose their methods do you wonder why they are so negative about me. They want your money. They don't want you to know the truth. Perhaps your own stockbrokers don't even know these things.

"A year ago, I attended Wade Cook's Wall Street Workshop™. As a former stockbroker and an active stock trader, I was very skeptical that Wade Cook's workshop would enhance my trading skills. But guess what-I discovered that I was one of those stockbrokers that "didn't get it." Sure, I knew a lot about the stock market, but I was unaware of the numerous financial strategies that have literally changed my life. I now

*realize that I can do the very things taught
at Wade's workshop for the rest of my life.
Could I have gotten this information as a
stockbroker? I don't think so."*

*~Frank Leuck (Was a student who became
a Wade Cook Seminar Instructor)*

So where are you in all of this? You're
either in your accumulation, maintenance, or
retirement phase of your life. The odd thing is
there are no set age periods. I'm amazed that so
many older people are once again learning new
things and doing our strategies. They want more
increased income and that's where we deliver big
time: Cash Flow, Cash Flow, Cash Flow. Bam, a
home run. Four runs and we're still up to bat.

I wanted to create a course that really gets
results. In fact, I wanted to make sure we stick
with our students, with an online Internet tutorial service-to continue to show, discuss, explain, explore. The service is called the Wealth
Information Network™, or W.I.N™. Find us at
wadecook.com.

To help you, we have an incredible home study
course, <u>Zero to Zillions</u>™, with 16 cassettes, a
video, and a second video (Wall Street Workshop™
primer) and workbooks. We have our two-day experiential learning formatted Wall Street Work-
shop™ where we all learn to walk the walk.

It's a complete package. I wanted to put together the most effective system of learning
ever designed-one which could cost $100,000 if
you don't attend. I know that sounds crazy, but
look at the following testimonials.

*"I feel very grateful that I became aware
of [Stock Market Institute of Learning]
through a friend and my brother-in-law early
in 1998. Prior to that time my investing*

experience was mainly through no-load mutual funds making about 10 to 15% per year.
Now, using my favorite strategy of selling
puts, I've been making more than that per
month. In fact, I made considerably more
money in the last two months than I made in
a whole year from my previous employer as a
purchasing agent. One of my trades that stands
out is when I sold a Feb 145 put on America
Online 10 contracts for $13^1/_4$ ($13,250), and
bought these back seven days later for $2^1/_8$
($2,125) which is a net profit of $11,125
minus commissions.

I am now investing full-time at home
and loving it. I am able to spend more time
with my family and donate more money to my
church. Thank you [Stock Market Institute
of Learning] for helping to make possible
this positive change in our lives."

~Don Gubler, UT

Will you get the same results? Probably not.
That depends on you: your commitment, your chosen favorite method and a host of other events.
We're the coaching staff. We'll show you how to
bat better-how to stand, how to hold the bat and
swing, in short, how to improve your rate of
success. Then you go into the batter's box. It's
between you and the other nine players.

The two most important things in life are
good friends and a strong bullpen.

~Bob Lemon

To say this further: recently we sponsored a
singles/doubles program with a local radio station. We donated $100 for each single and double
the Seattle Mariners hit ($100,000) to the King
County Boys and Girls Club. Our radio spots spoke

of form and style and that hitting singles and doubles consistently wins games.

Point: The 1999 regular season is now over. The Mariners lead the Majors in home runs - by far, but we didn't even make it to the play-offs. It's back to the meter drop. Consistent profits with systems for safety, cash flow and peace of mind.

I'd love to see you at one of our Wall Street Workshops™. Right now we're including a double package. We have an awesome one day event called B.E.S.T.™ (Business Entity Skills Training™) all about Living Trusts, Nevada Corporations, the powerful Family Limited Partnership, Pension Plans and Charitable Remainder Trusts. This day is worth every bit of the $5,695 tuition. Everyone needs this course. Now it's included with the Wall Street Workshops™ Package.

We're also including the Zero to Zillions™ home study course ($695) and three months of W.I.N.™. That's over $900 for the W.I.N.™ package and worth up to $(__xyz__), well, you fill in the amount you make from continually using these repeatable income formulas.

Now here is the special of all specials. We want you to make it big time. We went into a top level marketing meeting but brought in our sales team, group leaders and some instructors, there we hatched a plan to put $10,000,000 into the hands of our students. That's $2,000 for 5,000 people. $2,000 off the tuition that can be used for an IRA or just to trade. $2,000 used properly could have the profits pay for the course. These 5,000 spots will go fast.

There are no promises of results, just a promise of solid quality information taught in a way which helps you generate monthly income. If it is cash flow results you need, then ask, "Is the stock market for you?" You decide. If you decide to turn it into cash flow machine, then let us help you do that.

$2,000 off the $5,695 Wall Street Workshop™ tuition puts it at a mere $3,695. Yes this still includes Zero to Zillions™, three (3) months of W.I.N.™ and our ongoing educational support. Also the companion rate is $3,695. I'll knock the same $2,000 off the guest or spouses tuition. Note: when I was writing this letter, there was a better companion rate (Combo Tuition) and a few more months of W.I.N.™ Call and see if this extra discount and bonus are still available.

If nothing else, at least get Zero to Zillions™ for a current discount price of $495. We've had a Zero to Zillions™, W.I.N.™ package available for $995. Please, do something.

When you read that many of our current students are referrals from previous students, what do you think? We hope you read in this satisfaction and excitement and that you too will be taken care of. Your needs will be met and you will gain value.

When you read the accompanying testimonials by average, ordinary people, what do you think? Oh, they can do it but not me. Or do you think, "Heck if they can do it, I can too." All I need is a little help, a few insights and education.

When we talk about our style of learning, does it sound right to you? Is there a better way to learn? Is the timing right for you? "Every 37 seconds, someone becomes a millionaire in this country."(Anonymous) When will it be right for you?

Baseball is democracy in action: in it all men are "free and equal," regardless of race, nationality, or creed. Every man is given the rightful opportunity to rise to

*the top on his own merits. . .It is the
fullest expression of freedom of speech,
freedom of press, and freedom of assembly in
our national life.*

> *~Francis Trevelyan Miller*

You've all heard of "income producing assets."
For most of you, you are your only income producing asset. And if your asset doesn't show up for
work, there is no income. Our workshop is about
creating and developing another grouping of assets which will produce the income you need to
live on. Assets with income, that's our style.

We are also aggressively dedicated to building families. For example, right now we include
a $1,695 Youth Wall Street Workshop™ (teenagers)
for FREE. Your youth can attend the adult class
if you choose.

*Our kids are a message we send. . .to a
time we will never visit.*

> *~Anonymous*

We simply want to help you write your own
success story and we'll stick with you until you
make it, singles and doubles, the "meter drop"
method.

We stand by ready to help. The next move is
yours.

*Success is so rare, because relatively
speaking, so few are willing to pay the
price to achieve it.*

> *~Wade B. Cook*

Maybe all your dreams won't come true, but let
us help you master getting at the extra income
you need.

Appendix: The All-American Pastime

When I was a small boy in Kansas, a friend of mine and I went fishing. ...I told him I wanted to be a real major league baseball player, a genuine professional like Honus Wagner. My friend said that he'd like to be President of the United States. Neither of us got our wish.

~Dwight Eisenhower

Stay positive. If you cannot actually take time out to attend the Wall Street Workshop™, or physically cannot do so, then at least get the whole two day event on video. It is a wonderful set. You will miss the actual live experience with current numbers and examples, but you will have a handsome, professionally done video set of the live course. However, the live class is great! Call 1-877-WADECOOK (Source Code SAS-00) to order your copy today.

Keep away from people who try to belittle your ambitions. Small people always do that, but the really great make you feel that you, too, are great.

~Mark Twain

Make Up Your Own

Well that about covers it. If one of these emotional reasons has not captured your attention, and if you have not seen how we can help. Then I suggest you make up your own emotional reason. You have your own emotional and financial needs. Again, I submit that our course is the answer to your cash flow needs. If you don't use us, whom will you use? What are the alternatives? I see none.

We have what you need. We purvey quality information for your results and for your benefit. Don't delay your success.

Success American Style

> *I want to give back to other people what Wade gave to me, which was hope.*
>
> *~Freddie Rick (Wall Street Workshop™ Instructor)*

Investing in the stock market involves significant risk. Do your own homework and consult with financial professionals before investing. Although the testimonials contained in this report are from actual students, your results may vary.

Guarantee

Okay, still not convinced? You question these testimonials in the special report? So what if we take the burden to walk the walk. Here's our incredible guarantee. Oh, we honor the 3-day right of recession law. But we go so far beyond that.

To understand this you'll have to understand what an annualized return is, even though we've dropped the usage of the annualized return from our current marketing pieces. Let's say you take $10,000 and create a profit of $3,000. That is a 30% return. What if you made $3,000 profit in one month? You now take 30% multiply this times 12 and get a 360% annualized return. Nobody has ever said that you'll consistently use the same $10,000 and make $3,000 every month, so why do we use it? Just for fun. It's exciting to see what your money can make once you put the emphasis on generating income the Wade Cook cash flow way.

It is exciting, and it shakes up people's traditional way of thinking. In order to get people thinking like a cash flow millionaire we have to get them to "un-brain wash" their heads-to literally quit thinking of annualized returns and start thinking of one month, or even two weeks trades.

Appendix: The All-American Pastime

Okay so here is our promise of "three." We will:

1. At the Wall Street Workshop™ or within 3 months

2. Show you 3 trades wherein Team Wallstreet earned a

3. 300% annualized return.

If we do not you can get your tuition back. Obviously you have to work with your broker for suitability and to do the actual trade if you want to make the money. That is up to you. We don't give advice, we help you learn these strategies. Also, note all of these trades can be paper traded to help in your educational process.

Again, I repeat this guarantee of "three" to get your attention and to let you know we are here to help. Also note: We check the in-class trades every now and then for both real and paper trades of 300% annualized and Team Wallstreet averages six or seven, sometimes more, right in class not to mention the extra three months.

We hope this not only eliminates some of your fears, but gets you excited to get going. . .

Tuition and discounts change. The prices mentioned here may have changed by the time you read this. Call 1-800-782-7411 for current specials, schedules, and availability. Remember the price is one thing, the value or benefits are another. Don't delay.